THE CAREGIVERS' JOURNEY

THE
CAREGIVERS' JOURNEY

When You Love Someone with AIDS

Mel Pohl, Deniston Kay, and Doug Toft

A Hazelden Book
HarperCollins*Publishers*

The following publishers have generously given permission to use extended quotations from copyrighted works: From "How it Works," *HIVIES Manual,* Copyright by HIVIES, 610 Greenwood, Glenview, IL 60025. From *Protocol for AIDS Education and Risk Reduction Counseling in Chemical Dependency Treatment Centers,* by Caitlin Ryan, M.S.W., and Mel Pohl, M.D. Copyrighted 1989 by ARC Research Foundation, 12300 Twinbrook Parkway, Suite 150, Rockville, MD 20852. From *Alcoholics Anonymous* (Third Edition). Copyrighted 1939, 1955, 1976 by A.A. World Services, Inc., New York, NY. From *I'm OK—You're OK,* by Thomas A.

Credits continue on page 238, which constitutes an extension of the copyright page.

The vignettes in this book are composites based on the experiences of people with AIDS and their caregivers. Any resemblance to specific persons or specific situations is coincidental.

FIRST HarperCollins EDITION PUBLISHED IN 1991.

Library of Congress Cataloging-in-Publication Data
Pohl, Mel.
   The caregivers' journey : when you love someone with AIDS / Mel Pohl, Kay Deniston, Doug Toft. — 1st HarperCollins ed.
     p. cm.
   "A Hazelden book."
   Includes bibliographical references and index.
   ISBN 0-06-255339-9
   1. AIDS (Disease)—Patients—Care. 2. Twelve-step programs.
I. Kay, Deniston. II. Toft, Doug. III. Title.
RC607.A26P64 1991
616.97'92—dc20
                                                          90-55811
                                                             CIP

RC 607
.A26P64
1991

     91 92 93 94 95 MCN 10 9 8 7 6 5 4 3 2 1
This edition is printed on acid-free paper that meets the American National Standards Institute Z39.48 Standard.

Contents

Contents

Acknowledgments

We wish to acknowledge the following people for their support, encouragement, good wishes, and love:

Kevin Kelly, Kekau Rosehill, Nancy Sherman, Craig Rowland, Ginger Maiman, Mairz Davis, Mary Ceynoa, Gary Hamman, Mike Thias, Cora Courage, Will Pretty, Rick Pilato, the Scott Dugan's, Hannah and Derek Kerner, Amy Pitt, Michael Queen Whitt, Betty and Claude Bauermaster, Sherry and Dick Colquitt, Milica and Patrick Flanagan, Mary Schwartz, Barbara Ciarlantini, Rich Horman, Steve Lebow, Jim Gordon, Mike Walas, Mr. David Bjone, Tommy Servin, Jay Beadle, Dan Bowers, Elliot Francke, Cindy West, Mark Lichtenstein, John Jonikas, Jerry Cade, Larry Bienemann, and Dorothy Mackie.

To Ellen Buxton Siegel and to Edie Stark, many thanks. Thanks also

- to our families: Irene, Sandra, and Randall Kay, and the memory of Joseph Kay; Eleanor, Phil, Janice, Jackie, Lisa, and Larry Pohl; to Joanne, for years of patience and support; to the memory of Don Toft, for the lessons in laughter, tears, and music.

- to Becky Post and Tracy Brownson for their patience and wonderful editing.

- to Shinzen Young, founder and co-director of the Community Meditation Center, Los Angeles, California, whose teaching influenced the formulation of many ideas in Chapter Eight.

- to our supportive professional colleagues and good friends: Claudia Black, Larry Siegel, Drew Mattison, Dave McWhirter, Caitlin Ryan, and especially, Ellen Ratner.

- to beloved children, Rachy and Sverkei.

We dedicate this book to all caregivers and people living with AIDS:

"Have a safe journey."

MEL POHL
DENISTON KAY
DOUG TOFT

A Note to the Reader

This book uses the words "we" and "our" when talking about the experiences of caregivers. Using such words helps the authors speak directly and immediately to and about readers. It also stresses the bond the authors feel with caregivers everywhere. Using these words, however, is not meant to imply that all caregivers have the same experiences or *should* have the same experiences. The journey of the caregiver is different for each person. Using "we" and "our" merely helps affirm the fact that caregiving is a universal experience. We are not alone.

Throughout the book, we use references to ideas from Twelve Step groups—primarily Alcoholics Anonymous. To those who know something about the Twelve Steps and Twelve Traditions, many terms in this book will already be familiar. Nevertheless, this book is for everyone, including those without a background in Twelve Step ideas.

PART ONE

MEETING THE CAREGIVERS

Prologue

Millie served the Chicken Kiev and dead white asparagus, a menu selection she'd obtained from one of the magazines with the smooth complexions she'd read earlier that week at the doctor's office. She had run her slender repertoire of dinner menus past her husband, Charlie, that week and was pleased to be able to serve him something different on this special day.

But neither she nor Charlie had much of an appetite. Their dinner had been delayed by the forty-minute, four-way telephone conversation among she, Charlie, their pregnant daughter, Charlene, and her husband, Odell. Charlene and Odell had decided not to come for Charlie's sixtieth birthday. In fact, they would not see Charlie for a while, at least not during Charlene's pregnancy.

Pouring some hot tea from a pot rainbowed with tarnish, Millie regretted not polishing the silver for Charlie's birthday. So much time was spent with Charlie in doctors' offices, labs, and clinics these days. And then she had to deal with his depression and despondency. The news from Charlene and Odell was shattering, but she knew it was her job to cheer up Charlie. She blamed herself for raising such an ungrateful, heartless daughter. She silently cursed her intractable son-in-law.

Millie assured Charlie that this spate of unreason would blow over, still remembering Odell's words: "We thought about this a long time, but our decision is final. We ain't doin' this to hurt Charlie, but to protect his grandkid."

Noticing an increase in Charlie's chronically pained expression, Millie quickly brought out two paper party hats and the birthday cake. For the past four months, since Charlie's AIDS diagnosis, she had become their Hallmark card, their Dale Carnegie, their Hazelden daily meditation, their Daily Word from Lee's Summit, Missouri. But now her heart hammered. She felt dizzy. More than dizzy: frightened and unmoored as she looked at Charlie in the paper hat, crying like a baby.

Was he thinking about drinking? Yes. Would he suffer a relapse? To Millie, at this moment, it seemed inevitable. And she felt powerless to stop it.

* * * * *

Dan was calling his friends Steve and Cordy. "Have you heard about the gay cannibal who served the most divine finger sandwiches at brunch? How about the new women's organization called DAM—Mothers Against Dyslexia!" Jokes aside, he was also calling to catch up on the past three weeks, to tell them about his and Mark's capital-W wonderful vacation, and to find out what they were doing for dinner next Friday.

Dan did not get a rise out of Steve. But in response to his query, "What's new?" he got a private Hiroshima: Cordy had pneumonia. He'd been taken to the hospital twenty days ago and had been on a respirator ever since. Cordy's whole family from Iowa was there, keeping their vigil, enduring the hospital tedium. Dan was devastated, but rallied enough to make plans to see Steve, who needed some rest from the hospital and relatives. He welcomed the opportunity to see Dan and Mark. There was little point in making a special trip to see Cordy. He was not responding.

Mark walked into the den just as Dan was putting down

the receiver. The room had recently been redone—to Dan's specifications. That's the way things had been since Dan's diagnosis with Kaposi's sarcoma: everything to Dan's specifications. Never Mark's. So it seemed.

The den was done in High Conran's: a lot of polished pine and softly satirical London-between-the-wars upholstery. The lamps were faintly industrial—a concession Dan had made to Mark, who would have preferred a room of chrome and glass. "I don't want to live in a giant microwave oven," insisted Dan.

Mark knew at once that Dan was deeply saddened. Tears welled in their eyes as Dan relayed the news.

"Cordy is buying the farm. Kicking the bucket. Going to box city," said Dan. Mark suppressed a smile at Dan's attempt at humor—as always, trying to make a joke of it. Mark felt sad first for his friend Steve, then for Dan, and finally for himself. He feared that one day he'd be in Steve's shoes, going through all these emotions, watching a loved one suffering, dying. Dan suggested calling off plans for the smart dinner party they were holding next weekend. "It just won't be the same without Cordy." After five years of sobriety and over one thousand AA meetings, Mark knew he really needed a meeting tonight. The meetings were his port in the storm.

* * * * *

Carmen was getting cabin fever in her semi-private room at the St. Joe's Hospital AIDS unit. She'd been there for almost two weeks, with a lot of time between visitors and meals to contemplate. She worried about her twelve-year-old daughter, Inez, who made daily visits to the hospital after school. What responsibility that girl shouldered! Carmen worried about her son, eleven months old, to whom she'd passed on the virus, and about her overweight, arthritic mother, Hermenia, struggling to care for the three of them.

Xavier, her former lover, was on Carmen's mind too. She hadn't seen him since their son's christening, and she was craving his affection. Carmen harbored no grudges against Xavier—even though he abrogated all paternal responsibility for little Xavier, even though he'd given her the virus.

And despite everything she knew about addiction, despite her Narcotics Anonymous friends and her sponsor, Yolanda, despite the fact she knew she'd be sorry, Carmen wanted to get high on cocaine, to forget that she was sick, in pain, perhaps dying. She wanted to escape—just for a little while. Carmen still loved Xavier and hoped that a rendezvous with him held the triple promise of a good high, good sex, and some commitment to help with little Xavier.

For a few moments Carmen was awash in thought about her ex-lover. The reverie was interrupted by her cousin and NA sponsor, Yolanda. She was encased in a yellow dress with fat white polka dots, making her look like a giant slab of Swiss cheese. Carmen told Yolanda she could not go on, that in spite of Yolanda's advice to do otherwise, she was going to see Xavier as soon as she got out of the AIDS unit. In fact, she was going to call him that evening.

Yolanda feared the consequences of such a call and visit. All her counseling, all her advice would go down the tubes. The two women argued in Spanish. They were as polarized in their views and values as they were in appearance. Carmen wanted fun, love, drugs, and relief in the time she had left. She needed to get away. Her mother and daughter could look after the baby. Yolanda—overweight, overwrought, underloved, and sensible—had a sense of familial obligation and kinship, and a foothold in the Twelve Steps. She knew Xavier and drugs were not the answer. She also knew that if Carmen relapsed, it would make everything worse.

In the past, she'd been able to convince Carmen. Now she felt talked out and helpless. She'd call Inez. Maybe the twelve-year-old could convince her mother to stop acting like a love-starved, drug-crazed, man-hungry adolescent.

Just then Inez walked in carrying a Big Mac and vanilla milk shake, her mom's favorite. She'd overheard the two women shouting from the moment she got off the elevator. The throbbing headache returned — the one that had plagued her since her mom got sick.

CHAPTER 1

AIDS:
What About the Caregivers?

Our vignettes dispel some of the myths about AIDS. To-day, no one can dismiss AIDS as a condition confined only to gay men in San Francisco and New York. AIDS is now a fact in the lives of many of us. It rings false to segregate the threat to "high-risk groups." Anyone who behaves unsafely is at risk of being infected. Some have even been infected without unsafe behavior, such as babies and people who've received blood transfusions.

AIDS clearly dominates the stories of Millie and Charlie, Dan and Mark, and Carmen, Yolanda, Inez, and Hermenia. And another force is at work in their lives: chemical dependency. What about the caregivers in these stories? How will their lives be affected by AIDS and chemical dependency?

Our job in this book is to raise that question: What about the caregivers? Much has been written and said about the lives of people with the chronic diseases of chemical dependency and AIDS, and the people who have one or both conditions. This has been helpful. There is much more we need to hear. In our speaking and listening, however, we've paid less attention to ourselves—the mothers, fathers, brothers, sisters, wives, husbands, partners, children, sponsors, and friends of people with AIDS—the caregivers.

In the field of chemical dependency, there has been some

progress in looking at people who care for the alcoholic or person addicted to other drugs. Today, Al-Anon, Alateen, Nar-Anon, and other groups exist for the loved ones of alcoholics and addicts [of other drugs]. Most of these groups take as their core some version of the Twelve Steps of Alcoholics Anonymous. Beyond these is a steadily increasing base of literature on codependence, an issue for the family of the alcoholic or other drug addict. The burgeoning movement of Adult Children of Alcoholics is also taking hold. Despite their diversity, all these groups have a common focus: the impact of one person's addiction on friends and loved ones.

Has a similar perspective come to our awareness of AIDS caregiving? Not yet. This is our next challenge. So far, those of us who care every day for a person with AIDS have no clear maps for our journey, no pamphlets from the Surgeon General, no feature stories on the evening news. Even more complex are the issues of AIDS caregiving when chemical dependence is involved. So we ask: What about us, the caregiver?

CAREGIVING—OLD AND NEW

Caregiving is as old as human suffering itself. In Western culture, many of the earliest models for caregiving come from the Bible. Ruth, the subject of one book in the Old Testament, is one. Ruth, her sister Orpah, and Naomi, their mother-in-law, all lost their husbands during a famine in the country of Moab. Naomi decided to return to Bethlehem, her native city. She fully expected her daughters-in-law to remain in Moab, put their suffering behind them, and return to their own families there. Orpah did so. But Ruth refused, choosing instead to care for Naomi and declaring these intentions:

> *Entreat me not to leave you or to return from following you; for where you will go I will go; where you lodge I will lodge; your people shall be my people, and your God my*

> *God; where you die I will die, and there I will be buried.*
> *May the Lord do so to me and more also if even death parts*
> *me from you.*[1]

The Bible also records the words of those who comforted Job, the tale of the Good Samaritan, and the example of Jesus himself, who restored sight to the blind, made the lame walk, and even raised the dead. These stories embody traditional values about caring for the suffering person: self-sacrifice, loyalty unto death, and many more.

Helping others is also one of the fundamental principles of all Twelve Step programs. AA's Twelfth Step says "carry this message to alcoholics." And in the chapter on Step Eleven in *Twelve Steps and Twelve Traditions*, we read the prayer of St. Francis:

> *Lord, make me a channel of thy peace — that where there is hatred, I may bring love — that where there is wrong, I may bring the spirit of forgiveness — that where there is discord, I may bring harmony — that where there is error, I may bring truth — that where there is doubt, I may bring faith — that where there is despair, I may bring hope — that where there are shadows, I may bring light — that where there is sadness, I may bring joy. Lord, grant that I may seek rather to comfort than to be comforted — to understand, than to be understood — to love, than to be loved. For it is by self-forgetting that one finds. It is by forgiving that one is forgiven. It is by dying that one awakens to Eternal Life. Amen.*[2]

With AIDS, though, caregiving enters a new era. By necessity, AIDS calls for new forms of compassion. That's because of the unique emotional, financial, legal, and social aspects of AIDS in the late twentieth century — many of which are new because AIDS is so new.

The need for caregiving is a constant in human history, but today, caregivers need new techniques to keep their compassion alive. Are we here to devote ourselves, like Ruth, to another, bound for all eternity? Can we restore sight to the blind or cure our loved ones of their illness? Can we live the perfect life of St. Francis? As caregivers in the twentieth century, we answer no. While helping others, we can still care for ourselves. As the basic text of Alcoholics Anonymous states, "We are not saints. The point is, that we are willing to grow along spiritual lines."[3] And when we give up the ideal of sainthood, we can actually care more efficiently.

THE TOOLS OF RECOVERY:
A RESOURCE FOR CAREGIVERS

That brings us to the main point of this book: *The ideas that guide recovery from chemical dependency can also help caregivers.* For over fifty years, since the founding of Alcoholics Anonymous and adapted programs, there has been a healing conversation about guilt, shame, fear, and anger among people recovering from addictions. Each of these emotions figure in the daily lives of people with AIDS and their caregivers. For that reason, we'll talk about AIDS caregiving using the language of recovery. That language comes from the tradition of Twelve Step groups, beginning with Alcoholics Anonymous.

There are strong parallels between recovery from chemical dependency and coping with the emotions of being a caregiver of someone with AIDS.

- Addiction to drinking reduces the alcoholic's life to an unmanageable mess. Each day the alcoholic lives with lack of control, lost opportunities, misery, and social rejection. For many, HIV raises exactly the same issues.
- As with practicing alcoholics and other drug addicts, people with AIDS cannot control the course and outcome of the illness; instead, they can often count on feeling isolated and afraid.

- With AIDS or chemical dependency may come loss of health, friends, family relationships, and jobs.
- Finally, like chemical dependency, AIDS is a chronic illness for which no known cure exists.

Each of these factors reshapes the lives of caregivers, whether it's AIDS or addiction that's involved. Through self-help groups such as Al-Anon, the tools of recovery have been successfully applied not only to addicts and alcoholics, but to their caregivers. We think the same ideas can work powerfully for AIDS caregivers as well.

To make this point more clear, we focus on Mark, Yolanda, Inez, Millie, and the people they care for. Throughout the book, their stories appear as vignettes at the beginning of each chapter. Charlie and Carmen are recovering from chemical dependency and living with AIDS. Mark and Yolanda are caregivers as well as recovering people. And some, such as Inez and Millie, are neither chemically dependent nor living with AIDS; they are, however, primary caregivers. Our goal is to see how the tools of recovery might apply to their lives – especially for the caregivers.

The people in our vignettes have contrasting stories; their lives demonstrate the full impact of AIDS on our society. Charlie, the man with AIDS and alcoholism we met in this chapter, was infected with HIV through a tainted blood transfusion. Still, he has been accused of being gay or promiscuous – even though he claims he's been in a mutually faithful, heterosexual relationship for twenty-five years. And he thinks of drinking again. Millie, his wife and primary caregiver, grows more and more hopeless until she's able to admit her own powerlessness and turn to Al-Anon for help. Mark's response to a close friend getting sick triggers fears about his and Dan's future. Mark turns to the support of a Twelve Step program to help recover balance and acceptance. And Carmen's AIDS and drug addiction team up to make her feel totally out of control – powerless.

The stories we tell are about powerlessness, unmanageability, and stigma. In this book, we apply lessons from that experience. As our reference point, we'll apply a model of codependence to the situation of AIDS caregivers. In each case, our focus is on the hearts of the wife, the husband, the lover, the child, the sponsor, and the friend of the person with AIDS—the caregivers.

This book is really for all caregivers. We look specifically at those who care for people with AIDS. Even so, the ideas and techniques included here can be used by anyone who acts as a caregiver. This is true no matter what health condition affects his or her loved ones. In each case, the language of recovery is universal; it speaks to us all.

CODEPENDENCE AND CAREGIVING

One of the key issues in recovery is learning to deal with codependence. Codependence hinders our ability to care. Once we understand the pitfalls of codependence though, we can see our roles as caregivers more clearly.

What is codependence? It occurs when loving and caring for the other person become a necessity, an obsession, a preoccupation. The desire to help can become a desire to control—especially when our lives center on the feelings, the pain, and the health of the people we care for. In short, we become "other" focused rather than self-focused.

In this case, we constantly feel responsible for what happens to another. We discount and even deny our own life and our own needs. In fact, codependency is characterized by feelings of low self-esteem. Millie says, "I need to be everything to Charlie, but I feel like nothing. I've got to do more." Mark is certain that he must make sure that Dan wants for nothing. And how can Inez go through adolescence while tending to the needs of her ailing mother, Carmen, and her brother, little Xavier?

In *Codependent No More*, Melody Beattie defined a codependent as "one who has let another person's behavior affect him or her, and who is obsessed with controlling that person's behavior."[4] As Beattie points out, this condition is becoming so widely known that codependent jokes are even emerging: "Did you hear about the codependent wife? Each morning, she wakes her husband and asks him how she's going to feel today."[5]

Robert Subby, another therapist with a special interest in codependence, offers a complementary perspective on this topic. Subby defines codependence as an "emotional, psychological, and behavioral condition that develops as a result of an individual's prolonged exposure to, and practice of, a set of oppressive rules."[6]

Subby goes on to list some of the oppressive rules that work with codependence—in this case, in the family of an alcoholic:

- Don't feel or talk about feelings.
- Don't think.
- Don't identify, talk about, or solve problems.
- Don't be who you are—be good, right, strong, and perfect.
- Don't be selfish—take care of others and neglect yourself.
- Don't have fun, don't be silly, or enjoy life.
- Don't trust other people or yourself.
- Don't be vulnerable.
- Don't be direct.
- Don't get close to people.
- Don't grow, change, or in any way rock this family's boat.

These rules commonly spring from obsession with a sick alcoholic or other drug addict. And it makes sense for people to develop such rules when they feel afraid, ashamed, and out of control. We can see AIDS caregivers also feeling shame, fear, and loss of control. This is especially true when they become obsessed with a person with AIDS.

Timmen Cermak, M.D., has given us still another lucid explanation of codependence. Writing about adult children of alcoholics, Cermak compares codependence to Post-Traumatic Stress Disorder. Originally, this was a condition described in men who were soldiers in combat—most recently, in Vietnam veterans. But, according to Cermak, something like Post-Traumatic Stress Disorder can happen to any person who experiences ongoing trauma that's outside the range of normal human experience. Living with a chemically dependent person, he feels, is such a trauma—especially for children.

Even as those children grow into adults, a single event can "trigger" memories of that trauma, unearthing their buried pain. Cermak calls this "re-experiencing the trauma":

> *For children from chemically dependent families, the trigger can be almost anything: the sound of ice clinking in a glass, an expression of anger or criticism, arguing, the sensation of losing control, etc. The survival behavior they know is active codependence: focusing on others' needs to the exclusion of their own, feeling inadequate, exercising even greater amounts of willpower.*[7]

Cermak goes on to say that codependent behavior also has three other aspects.

- First is "psychic numbing," or shutting off from feelings.
- Second is "hypervigilance," constantly watching the surroundings to detect danger. That means never letting our guard down, never feeling safe.
- Third, there's "survivor guilt": wondering how and why we escaped the trauma—and feeling guilty about it.

So growing up with an alcoholic or other drug addict may lead to behavior we see in the veterans of war. In many cases, the dynamic is the same: long-standing exposure to uncertainty, pain, or even death.

Let's relate Cermak's ideas on codependence and Post-Traumatic Stress Disorder to AIDS caregivers. Caring for a person with AIDS can be one form of traumatic stress—similar to living through combat. The same uncertainty is ever-present. So is the long-standing exposure to pain and the possibility of death. And as with Post-Traumatic Stress Disorder, subtle events may trigger our emotions. These triggers will be different for each of us: the sound of labored breathing, a cough, the mention of AIDS on TV or in news headlines, or even hearing the word out of context, such as *"aid* to the Contras in Nicaragua."

We also experience psychic numbing to close out our feelings. We may do anything to block the pain, if only for a little while. Hypervigilance is a factor too. For example, Inez's constant fear is that her mother, Carmen, will develop a killing infection or turn to drug abuse. And for those who feel we're losing a loved one to AIDS, there's survivor guilt. *Why not me?* thought Mark. Millie, the daughter of an alcoholic father, wonders, *Why did I grow up sober and physically healthy, while my father died addicted and out of control? And now Charlie has AIDS—why not me?*

Codependence in the AIDS family mirrors codependence in the alcoholic family. We can suffer emotionally from the presence of AIDS in our loved ones much like the person who lives with an alcoholic or other addict. That suffering is real and is intensified by two kinds of relationship problems: trying to control our loved ones' lives and well-being, and basing *our* serenity on *their* serenity.

The Dangers of Numbing Feelings

Our purpose in talking about codependence is not to label, judge, or point a finger at anyone—especially at ourselves. Rather, understanding codependence has three goals:

- First, to help us become more aware of how we act as caregivers. We want to know what works and what doesn't. We want to know what really helps.
- Second, we want to nurture ourselves—in essence, to build our self-esteem—as we nuture another. Certain behaviors have been described as codependent; as we learn about them, we may see them in ourselves.
- With this awareness, we can move on to a third goal: changing the behaviors in ourselves that we don't like or that don't work. Promoting such change is the purpose of this book.

So much of what has been called codependence has one purpose: to block out feelings, to numb the pain. This is the "psychic numbing" Cermak talks about. Numbness, though not comfortable, may actually seem better than pain. And yet, numbness has its own flavor of discomfort. The experience is like having pain in your legs and sitting for a long time in an uncomfortable position until your legs go to sleep. Your legs, in fact, may become so numb that it feels like they're not really there—a temporary anesthesia; the pain is gone. But the numbness also causes a temporary paralysis of the legs; it prevents you from moving and is quite unpleasant.

Now what happens when you shift positions and the feeling in your legs starts to return? First, you feel a series of prickly, unpleasant sensations as the blood starts circulating again. Then, the original pain returns—the pain that was there all along. What's more, that pain may have only grown more intense while the numbness hid it. What's gained is some temporary relief, but, in fact, numbing the leg may lead to worse injury since we're unaware of the way it feels and might further damage an injured extremity.

It's much the same in the realm of feelings. Numbing ourselves to emotional pain may give us temporary relief. At the same time, while we bury the feeling, the pain could grow stronger and take root. We might become psychologically paralyzed, unable to move forward emotionally. And this may continue until we confront the source of our pain.

What's called for is carefully watching this process. Creating numbness is sometimes useful. After all, numbness enables surgeons to perform painful operations painlessly, and thus, to save lives. Likewise, it's useful for us to take respites from the painful emotions of caregiving. Through it all, we want to stay aware of the dangers associated with numbing feelings. We want to make sure that temporary relief does not lead to worsening the underlying condition.

BEYOND CODEPENDENCE: INTERDEPENDENCE

Codependence is a controversial topic. It's been the subject of much media hype, sensation, and superficial discussion. We do not wish to be mired in the arguments about what codependence means. Our aim is only to relate insights from the field of chemical dependency to the experience of loving a person with AIDS. Through it all, our goal is to care with compassion and strength – without losing ourselves in the process.

In addition to *codependence,* two other words are helpful in thinking about caregiving. The first word is *independence.* This is the opposite of codependence. When we speak of a person as being independent, we could also say that person is aloof, detached, or alone. If we act independently, we're attending to our own needs while ignoring the desires of others.

The second word is *interdependence.* With the following words from *The Prophet,* Kahlil Gibran was speaking of interdependence:

> *Sing and dance together and be joyous, but let each of you be alone, even as the strings of the lute are alone though they quiver with the same music. . . . And stand together, yet*

> *not too near together. For the pillars of the temple stand*
> *apart and the cypress grow not in each other's shadow.*[8]

Interdependence is the art of loving without being consumed. It is the art of caring for another without denying ourselves. It implies attending to another's needs while keeping our own needs in view. Other words for interdependence include feeling connected, in touch, engaged, or caring. As such, interdependence means gaining a sense of joy and serenity that *includes* the person we care for, but not *depending* on that person. As caregivers, interdependence can be our goal.

One More Note About Terms

We've used the word *detachment* to describe the state of being alone or isolated. This term implies a stepping back, a withdrawal from involvement, a shifting from involved participant to passive observer.

Even so, there are useful degrees of detachment. As we see in Chapter Eight, detaching from strongly negative feelings—sadness, shock, anger, fear—is one useful way to loosen the grip of those feelings. Once in awhile, it helps to step back, observe what's going on inside us, and suspend our judgments.

To this degree, detachment is a healing response. Carried to an extreme, however, detachment could lead to stifling, ignoring, or "stuffing" feelings. Eventually, these isolate us from others and hamper our ability to care. Again, our aim is to detach only to a certain degree—to the point where we move from codependence to interdependence. It is important to know that it's possible to give to others without being codependent. Some people fear codependence so much that they apply the label to *any* caring act.

Mark, for example, administers medication to Dan. This is an appropriate act because Mark runs a pathology lab; he has medical training. On the face of it, we cannot label such an act as codependent. Before we can apply any label to this behavior, we must look at more. We must keep in mind the whole context of their relationship over a long period of time. If Mark bases his sense of well-being on Dan having a positive response to the medication, this could be a sign of codependent behavior.

In addition, we want to avoid confusion about the labels of codependent, independent, or interdependent. These terms are only shorthand words for certain kinds of *behaviors*. Such words do not describe everything about a person. They cannot refer to a fixed, unchanging identity. Instead, these terms refer only to a "snapshot" of one person's action in one time and place.

So when Millie takes over Charlie's calendar and makes his medical appointments for him, we can say she's *behaving* in a codependent way. Nevertheless, it would be off track to say, "Millie is dependent," or "Millie is codependent." Any person is capable of a wide range of action. Some of those actions may express codependence; other actions may express independence. But in any case, our words are more accurate if they refer to the action, not the person.

PURPOSES OF THIS BOOK

What This Book Is About

Everything we say in this book draws from three basic ideas:

1. We can usefully speak of caregiving as taking place in stages. And within each stage, certain events commonly occur. Knowing in advance about these stages and events can help us prepare for them. In Part Two of this book, we explain each stage in detail: discovering, adapting, coasting, and colliding with AIDS.

2. By using certain strategies, we can cope with the painful aspects of caregiving in positive ways. More specifically, we can work through different phases in our response to AIDS: learning the facts, working with our feelings, and taking appropriate action. And we can work toward acceptance: attaining a deep, abiding sense of serenity and spirituality. This is our focus in Part Three.

3. Knowing about stages and phases of coping allows us to choose how we'll live our life, one day at a time. We cannot fully control the course of AIDS or the outcomes of treatment. Nor can we control other people's responses—their fear, anger, or rejection of our loved one with AIDS. Yet, we can decide how we *respond* to these events while holding on to our serenity.

That is our final freedom. Up until now, caring for someone with AIDS may have forced us through certain stages. Changing our responses and taking appropriate action, however, allow us to determine what the next stage in our life will be.

In our work with people with AIDS and their caregivers, we've often wished that there was a comprehensive guide to the caregiving experience. This would be a kind of "owner's manual" for caregivers, much like the manuals that come with new cars. Think about what's usually included in these manuals: details of how things work; notes on how to maintain the car and keep it in good running order; clues as to what can go wrong, warning signals, and what to do about them.

This book is essentially meant to be a guide to caregiving. By learning about stages, we can know something about how caregiving works. And by increasing our choices and learning about the phases of coping, we will be able to preserve our emotional health. And in this book we discuss clues, warning signals, and solutions that can help us do that.

Happily, there are landmarks on the caregiving journey. Other people are on this path, and some have gone before us. We can learn from them. There's no reason to feel alone or go into the caregiving experience "cold." There is help, there is guidance, and these can be ours if we take them.

How These Ideas Can Change Our Life

By applying some basic ideas, we as caregivers can experience positive change. What specific changes do we aim for? One is *identifying with others.* People report a common reaction when first encountering the material covered in this book. This reaction is identifying, recognizing another person's experience as their own.

This is central to the fellowship experienced in a Twelve Step group and in AIDS support groups. As members hear each other tell the stories of their lives, they're likely to make these statements:

- "That never occurred to me."
- "I didn't realize that could happen."
- "This is more complex than I ever thought."
- "I recognize those feelings."
- "I've felt like that and thought I was the only one."
- "That's my story."

This is useful to us as caregivers. By seeing the similarity in our stories, by learning what others have gone through, by hearing their stories, we can be better prepared to cope. By knowing the landmarks in the caregiver's experience, we'll feel more comfortable in this territory.

In doing this, we can accomplish another change: *to alleviate negative feelings.* We can begin to do this by naming, describing, and detaching from negative feelings in a way that heals. By learning a map of the stages in caring for someone with AIDS, we reduce uncertainty, confusion, and fear. We will also learn specific techniques for working with feelings.

In addition, we can *learn and develop caregiving skills.* The art of caregiving is the art of interdependence. It's a delicate, often precarious balance: being involved and keeping perspective; caring and yet being objective; spending time together and taking time to be alone; giving of ourselves and setting limits.

On one hand, caregiving means being open, positive, and available. It means increasing our confidence by learning about AIDS and acting on that knowledge. On the other hand, caregiving means admitting we don't always have the answers or know what to do. It means admitting our fears, taking time for ourselves, and getting help when we need it.

In doing these things, we give ourselves an empowering gift: freedom from perfection. As caregivers, we will take many actions to help the people we love. At times, what we do may hurt others and ourselves—even if we act with good intentions. And some of our actions truly will help. They will soften us, heal us, and help us forgive.

This is all part of our journey. Some of our words and deeds will hit the mark; others will fall short. That's okay. Caregiving means balancing opposites, and the line between them is never sharp and straight. Our path through the stages of caregiving will be full of curves. We may collide with obstacles and wonder how to proceed. We'll come to full stops, try detours, and even retrace our steps. No one can be a perfect caregiver every hour, every day. We need not ask this of ourselves.

Along with gaining knowledge and skill comes another change: *increasing choices,* finding alternative ways to respond to an event. Choices enable us to recover from the painful aspects of codependence, such as fear, anger, guilt, shame, and anxiety. We'll discuss choices more thoroughly as the book unfolds, especially in Part Three. Our goals in making choices are to attain serenity and define our own spiritual lives.

A NOTE ON THE APPENDICES

In order to understand the processes described in this book, it helps greatly to know certain things about AIDS. Many caregivers may already have mastered this material. For those who wish it, however, we've summarized key information in Appendix Three. Also included in the appendices is a list of recommended materials on AIDS and caregiving, a list of the Twelve Steps of Alcoholics Anonymous, and a list of the Twelve Steps for people with HIV illness.

CHAPTER 2

Yesterday

Charlie was the son of an old southern family, a once aristocratic clan that, instead of floundering in Faulknerian funk when it ran out of money, simply blended with good-natured resignation into lower middle class. He was thirty-two years old, single, with a spreading waistline. Charlie's line of work was selling; he sold refrigerators to restauranteurs and florists. He favored as friends fallen daughters and prodigal sons of the South, but could never bring them home because he still lived with his parents. They were devout Baptists.

On those occasions when he'd come home late from an evening of drinking and debauchery, and he had the misfortune of being greeted by his mother in the living room, he'd get a taste of hell's fire and brimstone from her accusing glances and sharp admonishments. "Agents of the devil" and "tools of Satan," were favorite phrases to describe her son and his friends on these occasions. Charlie's parents strongly disapproved of his drinking—but what could they do besides lecture? They weren't ready to throw out their own child. He was, after all, holding down a good job and paying them rent. And he only got drunk two or three Saturdays a month.

His parents were relieved and delighted when Charlie announced his engagement to Millie, a neighbor girl of sense, stability, and sobriety. Charlie had seen her in the neighbor-

hood before. One day, while both were walking their dogs in the park and the leashes got tangled, he noticed her good shape and her flaming red tresses. They were red and fiery, like plantation curtains the night they drove Old Dixie down. The dogs began to do immodest things to each other, and Millie's cheeks, the camellia color of a natural born red-head, suddenly pinked the color of an August peach. "Angus, you be a proper gentleman," Millie scolded her Airedale. And that was the beginning of Millie and Charlie.

They'd rendezvous every evening Charlie was in town. The romance was not like Dante's seeing Beatrice on the bridge; no, love was a long time coming. They really never dated. Charlie's way of courting Millie was to meet her in the park and to send her flowers. He gave Millie much floral attention. To her house came spikes of lemony gladioli, thick bouquets of asters, mums like emissaries from the sun. Millie's house was jammed with flowers; he gave instructions to his florist clients for the full treatment. There were imposing bouquets of tiger lilies and modest sprays of violets. There were branches of willows rising out of fresh moss and arrogant orchids displayed one at a time in little hooked vials. They brought her warmth and cheer.

Life as a child and young teenager for Millie was difficult. Her mother died when she was thirteen, and the burden of running the household and raising three younger brothers rested with her. One of her brothers was mildly retarded and needed extra care and attention. She'd go out of her way to cover up his mistakes, breakages, blunders, or battles with neighbors. She was always smoothing things over. Back in the forties and fifties, people's consciousness had not been raised regarding the retarded or the mentally ill. Consciousness not only needed raising, it needed excavating.

So she fought a lot of battles because of this particular brother who had become her favorite. She also had to look after her father, who had found solace and comfort in the bottle after his wife's untimely death. Her father's depression got worse when another son was hit by a streetcar and had to have his left leg amputated. Millie nursed this brother and ministered to her father, and it seemed that she would never have a life of her own. Her only outlet would be walks to a nearby park with the family dog.

The first years of marriage were blissful, but then Charlie's weekend drinking spilled into the weekdays. As the drinking got heavier and heavier, there were missed days at work, and Millie covered up for Charlie. She had to save face. There was some ugliness, some physical abuse, and a lot of yelling. Millie had hoped that having a baby would change Charlie, would make him more responsible. But the day Charlene was born, Charlie went out and got drunk with friends at a bar—to "celebrate" and, of course, pass out the obligatory cigars. He also filled Millie's hospital room with bouquet after bouquet of flowers. "I can only imagine what I would have gotten if I had given Charlie a boy," said Millie to her aging father.

Charlie, Millie, and little Charlene Griffin led an ordinary, run-of-the-mill, middle-class life. But Charlie was clearly alcoholic. Constant pressure from Millie and his parents finally pushed him into AA, and this program proved successful. There was only one relapse, when Millie gave birth to a stillborn son. Afterward, she had to have a hysterectomy. The night of the hysterectomy Charlie went out and got drunk. Other than that week of relapsing, he stuck to his program.

Millie was able to guide Charlie, to lead him to the path of sobriety. She was that classic paradox that is a Texas woman: steel coated and cream. While she cared for Charlie and Charlene, her primary family, she would make a point of looking in on her father and her brothers, who still depended on her.

Although Millie was frail as a porcelain shepherdess, she was also tough as nails. She survived her father's and two brothers' deaths, survived years of Charlie's drinking and abuse. *She survived his relapse. And now she had to face her daughter's betrothal to someone Charlie described as "having the intellectual capacity of a yam."*

* * * * *

It had been a month of new beginnings for Dan. First, the new position as feature editor at a daily paper—at age twenty-seven, the youngest person ever in that job. Second, the new apartment overlooking the Charles River, and third, a potential new boyfriend. The first bit of good news was expected and deserved, for he had been an outstanding journalism student at Harvard University. He'd apprenticed at that paper summers since he'd been sixteen. He was well liked and respected.

Dan had been living in an apartment in Boston's South End until two weeks earlier, when his aunt's will was probated. The woman, his great aunt and godmother in fact, was a septuagenarian of noble mien, bred to grand opera and table grapes out of season. She rolled her R's sometimes. As a child, Dan mimicked her odd pronunciations, a habit that lasted a lifetime for both and served as a continual source of amusement. Dan had been her favorite relative, so she left her condominium apartment and its furnishings entirely to him. The apartment on Beacon Street was a Maria Theresian folly of the eighteenth century and looked like the interior of the Schonbrunn Palace, only not as well kept up. The walls were covered with frayed brocade. At one end of the room hung a mildewy tapestry depicting a seventeenth century Austrian singlehandedly destroying the Ottoman Empire. Other furnishings in the rooms were old, heavy, and expensive. He was looking forward to redecorating.

Dan was effortlessly poised and unstintingly correct. He was like a brilliant creature trained in all the plenary arts one could cultivate with access to the proper circles and an abundance of clean folding money. Not a classically handsome man, Dan was still sensuous: thick, wavy hair, eyes oddly slanted, a hint of Saracen mixed somewhere back beyond his Italian heritage. He had a strong, perfect nose, full lips, the big flashy teeth of Latins and carnivores, a square jaw. His body was that of a natural athlete, and not of a Gym Dandy.

Dan also had the Italian genius for turning pin pricks into blood baths—something he'd inherited from his mother, Phyllis. He was a spoiled child in that he was raised in anticipating happiness. He was taught that happiness was attainable. And in the taxonomy of the day, he was a classifiable bisexual and a good catch. Being attractive to both men and women doubled his chances of having a date every Friday and Saturday night.

It was on one of these Saturday nights that he and his friend, Sheryl, met Mark. Mark was a defender of animals, a decrier of hypocrisy, a champion of beauty. The occasion was a fiftieth birthday party for a silver-haired epicene new neighbor, an old acquaintance of Dan's. Calder, the birthday boy, had served as a frequent escort for Dan's aunt. The arched eyebrows and accusing glances of strangers came not so much because of the couple's disparate ages as from his effeminacy.

Dan assured Sheryl that the party and the people would be fun. "It will be one of those successful parties where everyone talks and no one listens," said Dan. The living room was filled with gown and town types, and Dan and Sheryl quickly made their way to the dining room because they were famished. Sheryl gasped aloud; the dining room tables were stretched from wall to wall. It was an Aladdin's Cave of food and flowers, crystal, silver, and napery. Swans fashioned of ice cradled plovers' eggs in their depths. Chafing dishes blazed as though an arsonist had been turned loose. There was herring and chopped liver and Russian salad. There were grape leaves glistening with olive oil and vegetables in cold, curried mayonnaise. There was puff pastry and chocolate gateaux, strawberries and raspberries, purple figs and grapes of the palest green. There was cheesecake and pound cake, tarts and petits fours.

"I'd like to move in here," said Sheryl, "until early tomorrow morning."

"Fill a plate," Dan said. "Nobody in there will touch this stuff. They're too damn busy putting cocaine up their noses and pouring bourbon down their throats. The liver is gorgeous. Taste the liver, Sheryl."

Dan looked beyond the swan ice sculpture and spotted Mark. They actually spotted each other at the same time, and it was an electromagnetic coupling of eyes. The result was an early evening for Sheryl, but a rousing rendezvous for Dan and Mark, one which would eventually last a lifetime.

Dan found Mark to be manly, refined, and unaffected. High spirited, confident, and genial. Mark was mercifully bright and easy on the eyes, if not ruggedly handsome. He talked in italics. He had a marvelously mobile face, an expressive, graceful body, and flexible voice. The result was a Canterbury Tales—a rich and savory collage of human types and destinies.

Born in New England, Mark was the product of mixed-European ancestry, giving him a blend of stoicism and schmaltz. Mark was aware of his attraction to men as early as age seven. Yet he remained guilt-ridden and frustrated until his twentieth birthday. Then he finally gave in to what had become an uncontrollable urge: to be with a man. He was a contradiction of self-assurance and secrets, a troubled soul.

Mark had just moved in with his girlfriend, Stephanie, whom he was planning to marry. But after spending weeks and months with Dan, matrimonial plans were scotched. Seven months of intense fence-sitting was too much for the poor fiance. She could not wait for the prevailing wind to blow over Mark one way or the other. Mark knew his inclination; he enjoyed the life of drink and designer drugs. He envied Dan's joi de vivre. "I'll try everything in life except incest, pederasty, and folk dancing," Dan would say. Mark's evenings with his fiance consisted of TV, movies, marijuana, and hassling over his bisexuality. Evenings with Dan consisted of Byzantine dinners, theme parties, romantic meals at small ethnic restaurants, or drinks and coke with Dan's eclectic group of friends.

Stephanie finally gave him an ultimatum: He could see Dan, but must spend nights exclusively with her. The die was cast, and Mark knew then and there that he could not walk on both sides of the street. He'd have to choose a straight but less exciting life with Stephanie, and possibly children, or a life as part of a male couple with an exciting, captivating man. And with open eyes, he selected Dan.

Dan had done little to refurbish his aunt's vast apartment, and when Mark moved in, they redecorated. It was the beginning of life as a couple. But Mark warned Dan not to put too much money in construction or expensive wall coverings or draperies, because he wanted to move from Boston to expand the family's medical lab business to Arizona. After having lived through years of Boston blizzards and snowstorms, after having missed flights and even vacations because of emergency airport closings, after having scraped windshields for over ten winters, Dan too wanted out of Boston's Lappland conditions. But now was not the time. The new apartment and the new promotion had to be enjoyed.

So the men made a deal: leave Boston for Tucson or Phoenix in three years. And they made another deal. To love each other in their arms or in the arms of anyone they chose, till death do they part. In essence, they vowed to remain lovers to each other while having an unexclusive sexual relationship. "Wed, not dead" or "married not buried" or "the plural of spouse is spice" were their watch words. And in spite of jealous rages and drunken battles, the relationship worked and thrived during their three remaining years in Boston.

As the moving van rolled down Commonwealth Avenue

en route to Phoenix three years later, Mark and Dan jumped into their 1964 Jeep. They were driving cross-country to their new home. They knew that they'd both really miss their friends: the Apache types, the drug dealers, the Latin Quarter types, the Busby Berkeley cast of characters, doxies, and stage door johnnies, encircling their lives in Boston.

Phoenix was fun but a difficult adjustment. Their only "friend" was Loretta, a distant relative of Mark's, who was a part-time aerobics instructor and drug courier—or as they say in druggie lingo, a "mule." Out of boredom and a craving for friendship, they'd meet Saturday nights at Loretta's for dinner and drugs.

"My cousin isn't a very good cook," said Mark.

"I know. She can only make two things. Take it or leave it," quipped Dan. "She's the only person I know whose soup has to be eaten with pliers."

The Saturday night visits were such fun that they began visiting Loretta on Friday nights too. Bad suppers sometimes; good drugs always. Wednesday was Mark and Dan's night to reciprocate by having elaborate barbecues or lobster bakes. And there was Loretta, along with her beaux of the day, always bringing exquisite, uncut cocaine. So then it was Wednesday, Friday, and Saturday, which stretched into Sunday. And coke gave way to speed and weekends of debauchery in Phoenix, Los Angeles, San Francisco, or Palm Springs.

Mark and Dan prospered in their jobs—Mark in the lab, Dan in his journalism career. They made money and always made a point of holding drug expenses to $500 a month or under. They did this by cultivating "friends" who were generous with their drugs.

But too much became too much. Mark confessed that clients and "friends" or "tricks" had been visiting him during working hours and giving him "lines." He had always been buying a gram or two of coke a week, doing it up alone "for a lift." And, of course, there were his daily joints and the

Valium to "take the edge off the coke." And then, too, there were Quaaludes and "poppers" for sex.

One day, Mark announced he'd had enough — no, too much — of his drug-washed lifestyle. He was concerned that things were out of control. He was frightened, and as he took stock of his life, he realized that he had become quite miserable: depressed, angry all the time, restless, discontent. It was not anything specific in his life he was dissatisfied with — certainly not Dan or their life together. It was the drugs. He knew then and there that he had to stop. And for the first time in Mark and Dan's ten-year relationship, their bliss was threatened.

"Our social life and sexual life revolve around good drugs," said Dan. For Dan, the almost religious fervor with which Mark embraced sobriety seemed like an overreaction. Dan was capable of moderating his drug and alcohol use as he wished. But for Mark, his use of drugs and alcohol had become an addiction — compulsive, out of control, the cause of major emotional, and recently, physical problems. So Mark began to attend NA and AA meetings day in and day out.

Dan, at first, truly resented all the time Mark spent at these meetings — resented the new friends and new lifestyle Mark was embracing. Dan threatened to do outrageous things like try vegetarianism or join the Jim Jones sect or take up Zen Buddhism if Mark did not come to his senses. After all, Dan thought, Mark wasn't an alcoholic. He couldn't be.

But Mark knew different. He knew that two beers led to six, and that six beers led to more coke and grass and blackouts. AA became the order of the day and the order of his life. He became an AA regular, and for the next three years he lived soberly, cleanly, and happily. Dan got used to it and eventually saw the value of the meetings. Mark was changing, gradually and for the better.

* * * * *

Carmen's mother, Hermenia, came from Puerto Rico to New York City in 1974. She was running away from Juan, her alcoholic husband, who had physically abused her. He'd also sexually abused their two daughters, Carmen and Rita—mostly Carmen. Hermenia and the two girls lived with her sister, Margeurita, and Margeurita's daughter, Yolanda. The five of them lived in public housing in uptown Manhattan. Hermenia and Margeurita worked as underpaid dishwashers and kitchen assistants. They could barely make ends meet. On impulse, the women called Juan demanding that he mail money to support his family. He mailed himself instead.

After four months of living with and off the women, Juan got on welfare and was given an apartment for himself and his family. The drinking and physical abuse soon resumed after he had established himself, once again, as king of the household. And so did the sexual abuse. It all went on for years, taking its toll on Carmen.

Hermenia, Carmen, and Rita were emotional messes because of Juan's beatings, infidelity, blatant disregard for their feelings, and general financial non-support. They all knew he had other women, perhaps even another family somewhere in New Jersey. There were weeks when he'd never even show up, and no excuses were ever made. Juan was "entitled"; he was macho.

When Rita was sixteen she was killed in a motorcycle accident. She was buried six days before her father returned to the apartment and found out the news. No one knew how to reach him. Juan appeared remorseful and depressed for about two weeks. Rita had been his favorite. Usually while Hermenia was working, he'd terrorize Carmen. But while he was in mourning over Rita, Carmen got a reprieve.

Then one day, every trace of Juan was gone. Every stitch

of clothing, every momento gone. No warning. No note, no clue, and certainly no forwarding address.

By the time Carmen turned fifteen, she'd skipped more school days than she'd attended. She'd also discovered the East Village, men, and drugs. Hermenia saw the change in her daughter's moods. They were up and down, like a bell curve. She also began noticing new sweaters, a hair dryer, a portable TV, cosmetics, accessories, costume jewelry, and a big boom box. But it was not until Hermenia's niece, Yolanda, saw the aggregate of goodies that the picture became clear for Hermenia.

"Tia, where do you think all these things are coming from?" asked Yolanda.

"Baby-sitting money," said Hermenia.

"Who is Carmen baby-sitting for—the Rockefellers?" Yolanda was making sense to Hermenia as she spilled the beans. "Carmen is either selling herself or selling drugs or both, Tia," Yolanda said sadly and sternly. "We've got to help Carmen, especially if she's on drugs."

The two women were deep in conversation when Carmen walked in. Her hair was tightly pulled back and oiled, her lipstick red and smeared. She was so high her pupils threatened to overtake her irises. Yolanda spotted it immediately and she decided to show Carmen the "tough love" she'd been hearing about.

She knew the signs; she knew the symptoms, because she had had a bout with drugs for two years after her mother's death. Her mother had left her all alone, unloved, desperate, and wanting. A co-worker with the morals of Ninevah had convinced Yolanda that grass and speed were easy roads to a land of escape, beauty, and love: grass to help ease the pain of loneliness, speed to curb her hearty appetite so she could become slender and find a man.

Though she never injected drugs, Yolanda became addicted and lost thirty pounds. She spent the little money her mother had left her on more speed and her boyfriend, who

*was a con artist. She had come to her senses only after she
and the boyfriend were arrested—he for burglary, she for
receiving stolen goods. What followed was a stint at the
state-run drug rehab center and probation. Yolanda had
been going to Narcotics Anonymous since.*

*So Yolanda was no stranger to those things. She con-
fronted Carmen directly, accusing her of selling her body
and drugs. "Why are you on drugs? What are you running
away from?" Yolanda asked.*

*Carmen's reply was pointed. "I'm running away from
cockroaches and poverty. I'm running away from memories
of being raped by my lousy father and my own mother not
doing anything about it. Now I'm running away from being
pregnant. I'm running away from something I have growing inside me," cried Carmen, shaking.*

*And after six more months of promises and relapses, the
curtain fell. It was decided that Carmen would be hospital-
ized for treatment. She kept the baby, Inez, who was born
while Carmen was in treatment. Hermenia eventually quit
her job in the restaurant, assuming care of Inez while Carmen took some secretarial courses.*

*Yolanda was there through it all—the detox, the counsel-
ing, the birth. She was there for Inez's baptism; she was her
godmother. Yolanda was there for Inez's first day of school,
for grade school pageants, and plays. She was there during
Carmen's job changes and boyfriend changes; they came and
went like the Bay of Fundy tide.*

*And Yolanda was there when Carmen met Xavier at an
NA dance. If Yolanda had been critical of some of Carmen's
other boyfriends, she was unmerciful about Xavier. To
Yolanda, Xavier was a negative object from a bad family. He
was trouble and Yolanda knew it. Yolanda's NA sponsor and
friends, however, suggested that she was being critical because she feared losing Carmen and Inez. After all, if
Carmen married Xavier, who would Yolanda have to look
out for?*

Yolanda thought perhaps they were right about Xavier and she was wrong. He charmed Hermenia with compliments. He had a good rapport with Inez. He, Carmen, and Inez did things as a family: zoo, beaches, parks on Sunday. None of Carmen's other boyfriends had paid so much attention to Inez. No other boyfriend talked about marriage. All others had shied away from any commitment because they did not want the responsibility for a child that was not theirs or of a mother-in-law who needed teeth. So Yolanda resigned herself to the fact that she'd soon be losing Carmen, her best friend, and Inez, who was like her daughter.

Carmen and Xavier found a two bedroom apartment a few blocks from Hermenia. While marriage was not out of the question, Xavier saw no need for this step. So Carmen and Inez moved in with Xavier, who became like a husband and father.

Things went well for the first year until Xavier's older brother, Angel, was released from prison. Angel had been busted for selling drugs, and now he was back, offering his brother an opportunity for fast bucks and fast living. Carmen could either go along or fight it and be miserable. Either way, she'd lose. She chose to go along and quickly became hooked on drugs again. This time it was the deadly combination of intravenous cocaine and heroin known in the streets as "speedballing." Their lives revolved around selling and using—always looking over their shoulders. Inez was left alone too often, or had to lock herself in her room while Xavier, Carmen, and their friends shot up and "did business." She became isolated from her mother.

Angel was arrested and convicted again. By that time, though, Carmen and Xavier were too far into "the life" to turn back. The only time the family had hot meals was when Yolanda came over to cook. But she refused to come when Xavier was around. And he didn't appreciate her lectures, although he appreciated her good home-cooked meals, the clean sheets, and the clean apartment. Yolanda was always there to help. And once again, she was there to help when Carmen's son, Xavier Jr., was born.

The responsibility of another mouth to feed did not alter Xavier and Carmen's lifestyle. Inez quickly learned that she'd have to shoulder a great deal of responsibility for child care. Yolanda helped, of course, and enlisted Hermenia's help, which was often limited by bouts of arthritis.

Yolanda and Hermenia both grew more frustrated while Carmen, Xavier, Inez, and little Xavier grew thin and pale. As quickly as drug money came in, drug money went out— for more drugs. Eventually, Carmen discovered evidence that Xavier was cheating on her, and this caused a major rift. Once again, Yolanda was on the scene, urging Carmen to move away from Xavier, the drugs, and the two-timing. "He has more hot lovers than your children have hot meals," snorted Yolanda. "Why can't he bring home some groceries for you and the children?"

Xavier's latest dalliance with another woman was the last straw. Finally, Carmen saw that drugs and Xavier were not the answer. With support from Yolanda and Inez, Carmen packed up the few belongings she had and left him, stopping only briefly at Hermenia's apartment to kiss Inez good-bye. She climbed into the beat-up old truck Yolanda had borrowed. Carmen was on her way back to detox.

PART TWO

STAGES ON THE JOURNEY

Prologue

We see the caregiver's journey occurring in four stages:

- Stage One: Discovering
- Stage Two: Adapting
- Stage Three: Coasting
- Stage Four: Colliding

In this part of the book, we devote a separate chapter to each stage.

Within each stage, many caregivers and their loved ones share certain experiences. Stage One involves the discovery that a loved one has AIDS. With this discovery commonly comes a storm of negative emotions: shock, anger, denial, sadness, and more. And in each of the later stages, caregivers often find themselves with the same emotions recurring.

In Stage Two, caregivers and their loved ones move—at least temporarily—beyond those emotions. And in doing so, they adapt; they change. Such change reverberates at all levels of the self: thoughts, feelings, and behaviors. The aim is to somehow make things regular again, to establish a new equilibrium—even in the face of AIDS.

If Stage Two involves decisions to change, then Stage Three is living with the results of those decisions. In many cases, Stage Three allows caregivers and their loved ones to focus on things other than AIDS. They pick up and go on with daily tasks; they gain some perspective; they find some balance. And even though they're constantly aware that AIDS is present, caregivers may even see it with a certain matter-of-factness. We "keep on keeping on." For a time, we coast with AIDS.

Even so, coasting is not forever. Certain events may undermine the balance achieved in Stage Three. Our carefully wrought structure comes unglued. Things fall apart: A loved one dies; we face bankruptcy from medical bills; friends and family reject us. We call these collisions, and the task of overcoming them takes us into Stage Four. In the process, the old Stage One emotions—fear, anger, sadness, and all the rest—return. We may feel like we're back to square one in our journey, or even several paces behind. Moving past this stage calls on us to use the tools of acceptance discussed in Part Three of this book.

The idea of stages is useful and convenient. Thinking in terms of stages imposes a format on our journey. Reading about stages is like looking at a map or viewing a survey of the territory. It can bring some perspective and clarity into the tumult of our daily lives. The stages give us vessels in which to "pour" the contents of our experiences and to make sense of them. Also, they give us a way to talk about our lives as caregivers. They help us become aware of our thoughts, feelings, and behaviors. In these ways, they can promote healing and wholeness.

The idea of stages occurs in other fields too. With children, for example, we speak about stages of growth and development. In the field of chemical dependency, counselors talk about stages in recovering from addiction. And with death and dying, we talk about stages of grief. In the same way, the idea of stages can be applied to our journey as caregivers.

There is a danger in that any mention of stages, some people will use them like straitjackets. Some people may not go through the stages as described here. Others may worry that they're spending too much or too little time in each stage.

Concerns such as these only add to the issues we face as caregivers. And that's something we don't need.

To avoid this trap, remember that the stages are artificial. They are lenses through which we might view our lives. Other lenses exist, and they might serve equally well. Our list of stages points only to the milestones in the caregiving experience. And any such list is only as useful as it is helpful to our becoming more effective caregivers.

Not everyone will go through all the stages in the same way, in the same order, or in the same time. What's more, the stages we've laid out point to only one "cycle" in the process. In caring for someone with AIDS, we may feel as if we're going through these stages again and again. Or it might seem that we're stopping in the middle of a stage to return to an earlier one. When Dan develops a new complication from AIDS—pneumonia—Mark is awash with the shock, anger, and sadness that came with the original diagnosis of AIDS. At this point, Mark feels he's back to square one—back where he started, or even worse.

This is common. The stages are not a list of obligations or set of requirements. Let them be your servants and guides. They perform the same function as a road map to a city you've never visited. Once you know the streets and the major landmarks, you may not need the map anymore. You might even choose to explore new routes or stop at different points on the journey. We offer our stages as the same kind of tool. If they help your thinking, fine. If not, act on an old saying from Alcoholics Anonymous: "Take what you like and leave the rest."

CHAPTER 3

Stage One: Discovering— Learning the Painful Truth

Poking kumquats and wondering if Charlie would eat jicama, Millie flashed on the upcoming doctor's appointment. Charlie had been lethargic for months. Beyond lethargic. He had as much energy as a fly in January. Usually an early riser, he had been sleeping later and longer. When he was not being Willie Loman on the road, he'd sneak home during lunch hours for "power naps" that lasted two hours. At first Millie suspected that Charlie might be coming home to "sleep it off." She made a point of giving him a big hug and kiss during these matinee appearances, surreptitiously smelling his breath for evidence. She thought, "Thank God no booze! I don't know what I'd do if he started drinking again." Upon returning from work at five or six, Charlie would want to nap again and just stay in. Invitations were routinely refused and seldom extended.

The visit to Dr. Ratner was a follow-up to the one last week, precipitated by a call from Dr. Ratner's nurse. The blood bank from which Charlie received blood sixteen months earlier was concerned over a blood scare and had called all blood recipients to be checked for HIV. Charlie's doctor assured him that it was just a routine procedure and not to be concerned.

Millie hurried home from the supermarket to prepare a

light lunch for Charlie and to lay out fresh socks and underwear in case more undressing and examinations were necessary. She suspected this would be the case, because in the week between appointments, Charlie's ulcer had come out of the closet.

A little before three, Charlie and Millie arrived at Dr. Ratner's office. Millie sat opposite her husband. She looked at him intently. He looked skinny and nervous, like the last snake out of Ireland. Pale as a phantom tangled in lace curtains. Pale and panicky. Millie silently fretted as she sat calmly in the Eames chair doing her needlework, poking her needle in and out, looking like Madame Defarge knitting while the tumbrils rolled in the streets.

Charlie stared at the minimal art in the office. He felt trapped in the sterile airlessness of the waiting room, overwhelmed by a surfeit of pastels and understated good taste. The office had recently been redecorated by Dr. Ratner's daughter-in-law, an interior designer.

The nurse, short and gray, came to get Charlie and Millie. She asked if Charlie was okay, he was so pale. Moments later the grim-faced doctor walked in and shook hands with Charlie, whom he had known for years. He was the Griffin's family doctor. He had helped deliver their daughter twenty-four years earlier, and had been the family's physician since.

The news was not good. Charlie had tested HIV positive and all signs—lethargy, weight loss, night sweats, blurred vision, and thrush—pointed to AIDS. "You're full of crap!" shouted Charlie, "Let's get out of here Millie." Millie tried to calm her husband. The doctor and Millie protested Charlie's outburst, but he'd hear none of it. "AIDS is for queers and drug addicts, not God-fearing middle-class people!" Charlie shouted. He stormed out of the exam room, out through the pastel waiting room, and onto the street. He felt dazed and hopeless and went into a bar and had a double Scotch, and another, and another. He would not stumble home until twelve hours later.

Millie spent another fifteen minutes with Dr. Ratner, asking questions about AIDS, its transmission, and how contagious it was. She wanted to know about possible treatments. The prospects looked bleak. She left the office armed with literature, fearing that Charlie would be detouring at some bar.

Once Millie arrived home, she thought a hot meal of meat and potatoes would be best for Charlie now. She began preparing a lamb stew, his favorite. She cried as she peeled the potatoes. She, of course, blamed herself for Charlie's illness. Why did she ever pick Dr. Ratner as a family doctor? Why did she let Charlie get that blood transfusion?

Millie was well aware of the horrors of AIDS. She had read stories in Time *and* Newsweek. *She had heard the lengthy nightly news reports and she now heard the death rattle. Thoughts of imminent widowhood brought her to her knees in grief. She wept uncontrollably into her apron, and still, she knew that she had to pull herself together and be strong because Charlie could not face this without her strength. He was too sick, too weak, and too ashamed to face his own illness. When she finally gained composure and was satisfied that the stew was coming together, she decided to look through insurance policies. She wanted to make sure that Charlie's health insurance was all paid for and in order.*

She also wanted to check life insurance policies. The thought of handling his life insurance policies brought her to tears once again. Unpleasant though it was, she knew that she had to do this; her husband would simply not take care of these matters. He would deny that he had AIDS. He would behave as though whatever was troubling him would go away. After all, someone had to take care of these things. Millie, as always, nominated, voted for, and elected herself. She dried her tears. It was time for her to be sworn in.

* * * * *

Dan had suspected for months that the purple spot on his forearm was cause for concern. He had shown the spot to his friend Rowland in New York City a half year earlier. Rowland, a self-acknowledged hypochondriac, had for once correctly diagnosed his own Kaposi's sarcoma five years earlier and told Dan that in his unprofessional medical opinion, what Dan had was not an aggressive virulent lesion, but an old age spot.

"Vanity does not permit me to acknowledge the possibility of age spots," said Dan, momentarily disregarding the alternatives. It was months later when another "age spot" appeared and Dan showed Mark. Mark suggested a biopsy under a fictitious name. Hours were spent thinking of alternatives to John Smith. Dan and Mark met with their good friend and doctor whose professional opinion parrotted Rowland's: the spots didn't look like KS lesions. They were most likely age spots or benign skin cancers. The doctor did a biopsy of the one spot and rushed it to the lab. He'd call Mark with the results, rather than have Mark check the results himself.

The lab had several gay employees who loved to grind the gossip mill, and any inquiry about a lab result would arouse immediate suspicion. And such action on Mark's part, and subsequent suspicion on the employees' part, would pepper the weekend conversation in many circles. "Why was Mark in the lab? Why was he so concerned about the test results of Murgatroid Popoofnick, and who was Murgatroid Popoofnick?"

It was almost Memorial Day, and the cicadas in Phoenix had begun their lunatic parliament in the trees. Mark and Dan had been planning a long weekend in Ocean Beach, California, to escape cicada mating season. A buddy of theirs offered them use of his oceanfront apartment while he was abroad. Dan preceded Mark by several days and was unaware of the call from Dr. Maiman. The diagnosis was positive for Kaposi's sarcoma. Mark's heart sank. He didn't want to call Dan in Ocean Beach and break the news over the phone. This had to be done in person so he could offer comfort, so he could take care of Dan. A flood of emotions and feelings inundated Mark: shock, fear, panic, disbelief, grief.

Minutes after Dr. Maiman told Mark the bad news, a friend of Mark's called, and Mark felt the compelling need to share this news with her. She was a therapist and offered some comfort. He feared for himself—widowerhood looming. He feared for Dan—depression, disease, dissipation.

When Mark arrived in Ocean Beach, hugs and kisses and pleasantries were exchanged. The weekend was full of possibilities, but Mark's eyes said it all. Dan knew within five seconds that Dr. Maiman had called with bad news. "I'm dying, aren't I, Mark?" asked Dan.

Mark grabbed Dan, hugged him and began to cry. "I'm so sorry Dan; I wish it were me." He noticed Dan's expression. Dan wore grim lips and a far-away squint, both mute. "If I could take this away from you and put it on me, I would," continued Mark. "What are you feeling?" he asked.

"I'm feeling nothing; I'm numb," was Dan's response. He quickly added that he'd be all right, that he was worried about Mark and what effect this would have on his sobriety. He also said that this was their secret and that absolutely no one was to know.

"Uh-oh," said Mark with growing apprehension, "I told Pepper. She called two minutes after Dr. Maiman called with your test results, and I had to tell someone! It just seemed like the natural thing to do, to tell a friend."

Dan was enraged, "What right do you have telling people about my illness and my health problems, and even before I knew. That's contemptible. Your pathological need to share and emote to friends will make me sicker and drive me into the grave sooner."

A loud argument ensued for the next half hour about the pros and cons of disclosure. They were polarized, 180 degrees apart. Mark saw therapeutic value in telling everyone, and in immediately joining AIDS support groups. Dan, reared stoically and properly, had been taught that sickness was private, if not boring. It was nothing to be ashamed of, but discussion about one's illness was ill mannered, a big yawn, unnecessary. There were more interesting things to discuss with friends and acquaintances: Persian archeology, English madrigals, kell work, the National Enquirer.

The issue of "whose illness is it" created a Mexican standoff between the men, and, for the rest of the evening, it was the serpent in their defoliated Eden. Dan wanted to be alone, to think things out. He did not want to go out and enjoy the honky-tonk of Ocean Beach tonight. Mark, on the other hand, wanted total escape—escape from what was and what was to be. Having given up alcohol and other drugs two years earlier, he chose the only other form of escape he knew: anonymous sex at the bathhouse. He left Dan an hour after he had broken the news; he left for the baths.

For the next hour Dan was in a rage over his diagnosis. He felt angry. "Why me? I don't deserve this!" He was furious with Mark for telling Pepper and thought about leaving him. But after an hour, he emerged from the fury over his disease and his betrayal by Mark. Nowhere inside him was an explanation. He was convinced that there had been a mistake, even though he knew mistakes were seldom, if ever, made at Mark's laboratory. Such matters were too important to allow for any error. He knew Mark ran a very tight ship and had a reputation for accuracy and overall excellence.

As the rage subsided, denial was the main order of the evening. He perused his friend's bookshelves. His friend Dennehy was an interior designer for the fashionable of Ocean Beach and La Jolla. "Books are so decorative, Dennehy," he would say. The pickings were slim: Christmas with Liberace, decorative Reader's Digests, six volumes of leather bound Torts of California, and a three-volume biography of Charles the II, also known as Charles the Dull.

Meanwhile, in the halls of the bathhouse, Mark was awash in the experience of physical contact, anonymous and limited as it was.

For a little while, both Dan and Mark had managed to escape the unpleasantness, horror, and grief they knew was coming.

* * * * *

Carmen opened her eyes to a blizzard of cherry cough drops. Yolanda had just painted her fingernails and was drying them in the air while sitting on the hospital bed watching Carmen stir out of her restless sleep. Yolanda and Inez were talking about Christmas shopping, comparing consumer triumphs at various K marts and Woolworth's. Carmen had been rushed to the hospital four days earlier, Thanksgiving night. She had difficulty breathing and her forehead was hot. Since then, Yolanda had practically lived in the hospital, helping Carmen, holding her hands through the endless succession of blood tests, blood gases, respiratory tests, and hospital routines. "Do you want me to paint your nails, cousin?" Yolanda asked, still waving her hands in front of Carmen, drying her nails.

Carmen was in no mood to look pretty. She did not like hospital confinement. She did not like being linked to oxygen apparatus, nor did she like being sick, although she enjoyed Yolanda's attention. She smiled at Inez, exchanged endearments, inquired about school, little Xavier, and her own mother. Yolanda was in the midst of explaining that both she and Hermenia had taken off from work the next few days to be with Carmen and care for the baby, when Carmen's primary physician walked in. The doctor, impatient and cornstarched in arrogance, ordered Yolanda and Inez out of the room.

Carmen insisted they stay; they were family. The doctor studied Inez. Her face was pretty, self-conscious, but a pair *of unfortunate glasses disfigured her appearance, he thought. He smiled at Carmen. It was unnatural, forced, institutional. "I'm afraid you have AIDS, young lady. All tests confirm it. And you have the beginnings of pneumocystis pneumonia."*

Carmen felt light-headed, faint, confused. She wanted to escape—pull out all the tubes and run. High drama ensued. Yolanda began praying in Spanish, invoking a litany of saints' names, crossing herself frantically and fanatically. An even bigger cherry cough drop blizzard. Carmen looked at Yolanda and told her that if she was going to die, she wanted to go out partying. "I'm not going to wither away in some hospital room," she said. "As long as I have strength, I'm going to dance, drink, and party with my boyfriend," she shouted. Inez did not know which hysteric to comfort first—her mother or her cousin. Her head moved from side to side, as if watching a ping-pong game.

Both Yolanda and Carmen knew about AIDS: the dissipation, the pain, the shame. So many of their drug-using neighbors and friends were dead or in the very vestibule of death because of AIDS. Inez, on the other hand, was an unaware witness who tried offering consolation to the two inconsolable women as the dispassionate doctor looked on.

Inez went to her mother's bedside. She knew that her mother was needier and more helpless than Yolanda. Yolanda can handle things better than Mama, *she thought. And down deep, Inez knew that even she could handle things better than her poor mother.*

Mother and daughter reached out for each other and began to cry. "Mama, what's wrong? What did he say?" Inez asked, as Carmen was sobbing and repeating, "My babies, my babies." With this, Yolanda momentarily stopped her praying and began to cry. The doctor addressed Inez. "Your mother has a serious disease, and all people with this disease waste away and die. It's not pretty. You get it from drugs and sex." Half listening to the doctor's words and her own plaintive lament for "her babies," Carmen made a mental note: "Ditch this doctor. He's a pig."

She interrupted and drew Inez close to her. "Remember Luis Ramieriz in 12C? And remember Hector, how fat he was? Remember how sick they both were? Always going to the clinic or the hospital? Do you remember how skinny they both were before they died — especially Hector? Hector had those purple and black spots on his face and arms, and you asked me what was wrong with him? You remember? That's what I caught Mia." Carmen began to cry again. Inez embraced her mother and said, "I'll take care of you Mama. I'll be your nurse. And I'll take care of little Xavier too. Don't worry."

The doctor spent about two more minutes in the room going over a "what's next, what's in store" routine. Carmen asked no questions. She disliked the doctor from the outset, and now she hated him. She hated him for the bad news, hated him for being so cold and insensitive to her at what was the lowest moment in her life.

* * * * *

INITIAL RESPONSES

Shock, anger, fear, hysteria, sadness — these are the emotions experienced by Charlie and Millie; Dan and Mark; Carmen, Yolanda, Hermenia, and Inez. And the same emotions arise in most caregivers at the moment of discovery. This is the moment when AIDS reveals itself, when it steps out of the closet in the form of a diagnosis. Discovery ushers in Stage One of our journey.

Most often, discovery penetrates directly to the heart: our first responses in Stage One are usually at the level of pure emotion. In this chapter, we explore these emotions in detail. We give examples of each emotion. And we chart the life of these emotions — how they arise and develop.

Before looking at each of them in detail, we want to make several points about these emotions in general:

- *Each person's response to the diagnosis of AIDS is unique.* So are the responses of each constellation of family and friends. Certain emotions commonly make up this response. But by mentioning these emotions, we are not implying that caregivers will—or should—feel any of them. Nor do all of us experience the same feelings. We are simply reporting what many caregivers feel with the discovery of AIDS. Our responses will depend on who we are as individuals.

- *Feelings arise in different ways.* Some of them may surface acutely and all at once. Other emotions we discuss may arise later. It's also common for these feelings to come and go, to wax and wane, emerge and subside. The feelings we're about to describe often surface at the time of diagnosis and then recur at later stages of living with AIDS.

- *People can "replace" one emotion with another.* Some may express anger when fear is really the driving force in their response to AIDS. Or they may only be conscious of fear when the underlying emotion is grief and sadness. In short, feelings arise in dozens of ways, with different textures, combinations, and nuances.

- *The person with AIDS and the caregivers may cycle through these feelings together, or they can move through them separately.* This may happen differently over time. Early on, the person with AIDS and the caregiver commonly feel similar emotions. Both can identify denial, anger, shock, and disbelief. And both may feel themselves cast into a shadow area, blurring their ability to affirm life.

Even so, some feelings are unique to the caregiver. For Mark, these feelings surface later as questions that cut to the core: "Is it me?" he asks. "Did I give Dan the virus? Why him?

Why not me? Should I get tested? Is he going to die? Am I going to die?"

Millie asks: "What's going to happen to me? Charlie is sure he's going to go crazy, or become disabled, have pain, get sick, and die. Is he right? Are the same things going to happen to me? I've got all this to cope with, plus I'll have to nurse him. I'll have to spend all our money and give up my time. And after it's all over, I'll be alone."

With these points in mind, we move on to common Stage One emotions:

- Fear
- Anger
- Sadness
- Shame
- Guilt
- Anxiety
- Shock
- Denial
- Withdrawal
- Rehashing the Past
- Blame
- Piling Reaction on Top of Reaction

Fear

Caregivers commonly report fear. The basic text of Alcoholics Anonymous captures the nature of this feeling: Fear "was an evil and corroding thread; the fabric of our existence was shot through with it."[1] As with alcoholism, AIDS involves so much to fear (and realistically so) that it practically consumes us.

We can name several ways that fear arises in us. First, there's the fear that things will come apart, a profound uncertainty about what the future holds. This is fear of the unknown. We wonder what will happen to the people we're caring for. We may wonder about the future of our children, our parents, our friends, our loved ones. Like Millie and Mark, at a deeper level, we ask, "What will happen to me?"

With it may come the fear of abandonment, of being left alone. Mark asks, "What if Dan leaves me—through an extended hospital stay or through death? What will I do then? If he dies, how can I go on?"

"Is Mommy going to go away like she used to and leave me alone?" Inez asks, removing her glasses and wiping a tear from her cheek. To many such questions, we find no answers.

There's fear for our loved one's physical condition. *Will Charlie become disabled, incapacitated, blind, or disfigured?* Millie wonders. Closely related is a foreshortening of time, and that can bring a distinctive flavor of fear. The future narrows; we feel the weight of lost possibilities, lost dreams. As Millie says, "If Charlie dies, we won't grow old together. We won't see the turn of the century. We'll never see our grandchildren grow up, go to college, get married, and have families of their own."

Financial fears are just as real. "This is costing so much money," Mark says. "What happens if the insurance runs out or is cancelled, the money goes, and the bills keep coming in?"

Yolanda wonders, *What will happen if Carmen dies? Will I be responsible for Carmen's children: little Inez and baby Xavier? How can I afford to raise two little ones?*

Change in itself brings new fears. In our journey as caregivers, this fear can be profound. We fear change in our physical surroundings. Also, the person with AIDS may be confined to a wheelchair. Faced with this, we wonder if our homes will allow for that. *Can we adapt the house?* Millie thinks to herself, *The bathroom, the stairs . . . will we have to move out of our lovely home?*

Fear arises, too, over the sheer volume of work. "All the responsibilities we shared, now they'll be up to me," says

Mark. "It'll be twice as much work. Who will take care of the house, the dogs, the bills?"

With this is fear of embarrassment, rejection, and public exposure. Telling people about addiction is hard enough; revealing HIV disease can be even more grueling. We want to know what people will say about us and how they'll treat us. And we want to know that *before* we tell them about AIDS. We fear for our jobs. We fear rejection from our families and can become obsessed with what the neighbors think. Fear of losing even close friends is common at this point. Inez, already finding that children can be cruel when they hear of Carmen's illness, feels isolated, alone. And she fears that it will get worse.

Embarrassment is a common response to the diagnosis of AIDS. The question immediately arises, "Oh my God, how are we going to handle this information? Who can we possibly tell?" This is compounded by the dilemma, "Who *owns* the information about the diagnosis anyway? The person with AIDS? The caregiver? And which person decides who to tell about the diagnosis, and who *not* to tell?" As we see with Mark and Dan, this is already a source of conflict in their burdened lives. It will remain so.

Embarrassment arises over the threat of disfigurement too. Some conditions related to AIDS, such as Kaposi's sarcoma, cause lesions or other visible signs of illness. In Dan's case, "Will it show?" is the constant question. In fact, AIDS can literally be self-revealing. The condition may not permit us the luxury of keeping secrets. Dan finds himself hiding his lesions—going out less in shorts, or not going out at all. Mark notices this, but the change goes on, unacknowledged. Carmen gets so sick so quickly that all the neighbors know before Hermenia is able to think up an effective cover story.

As caregivers and lovers, we also fear for our own lives and health. *Am I next?* Mark and Millie wonder. *Will I develop HIV disease? . . . Do I have the infection? . . . Who gave it to him?*

. . . Did he give it to me? . . . Will I get sick? . . . All the things happening to him, will they happen to me? . . . Will I die?

Add to these the threat of lost sobriety. "Carmen will start using drugs again," says Yolanda. "She won't be able to stay away from the pills and dope now that she's sick—and the cocaine. All the progress she made, it'll be lost. I want to go get loaded too. God, I haven't had such thoughts for years." Millie's worst fears come to life too: Charlie drinks. And the downward spiral of his alcoholism makes matters much worse for both of them.

Carmen's thoughts run on similar lines. *People at meetings don't understand AIDS. We're supposed to be grateful for NA and AA. Are we supposed to be grateful for the AIDS too? I just don't care. I can't cope. I just don't want to deal with it, and I need something to fix the pain. Coke may help me feel better. I'll stop hurting, at least for a while.*

Anger

Another common emotion, with its many dimensions, is anger. Anger goes straight to the gut. It's a basic, primal emotion. Despite what we're showing on the outside, one part of us screams, venting rage: *No! No! No! How dare this virus invade my world. How dare it screw up my life.*

Often we first direct anger at the medical system. We may feel that doctors and nurses just don't know what they're doing. To us they can seem distant, far away—even afraid of us. What's more, we feel powerless to do anything about it. The people in our vignettes express it:

> "Dan took AZT and needed blood transfusions *every two weeks*," says Mark. "It was worse than dying. I wasn't allowed to visit him in the intensive care unit because I wasn't 'family.' After sixteen years together—not family!"

> "Why can't we get experimental drugs?" Millie asks, feeling her blood pressure rising. "And why doesn't the lung

> *specialist talk in words I understand? He really doesn't talk to me at all. Why am I afraid to ask him what's going on? Is it my imagination, or is he avoiding me?"*

> *"Why doesn't Carmen's doctor give her a medicine to help the symptoms?" asks Hermenia, Carmen's mother. "They should do something about her pain and her nerves!"*

That anger may expand into larger territory: toward society, institutions, and the legal system. This is "big anger." It uses a lot of energy because the pain caused by AIDS is so real, so concrete. At the same time, the "others" we're angry at are large, faceless institutions. Anger at them, besides frustrating us, may produce no real change.

"They found out about Dan's HIV disease," Mark says. "Now we may lose everything — our insurance, our income, our house. Cordy got fired; maybe I will too. And his parents sued to take away the house he owned with Steve. How can they possibly get away with all this? Where has his family been for the last five years? Don't they know anything about AIDS? Who do they think they are to discount Steve and Cordy's relationship?"

Another form of this is blaming the nameless other, the anonymous "they":

> *"It's the fault of those gays and addicts," Millie cried, to no one. "They started it — or maybe it's those primitive Africans or Haitians! I have to blame someone. And my Charlie got the virus through a blood transfusion. I could strangle the people who donate infected blood. Why isn't there more being done for people with AIDS and their families? Don't they understand?"*

> *"There are new drugs," protests Yolanda. "Why won't they let Carmen try them? The government was supposed to make sure this couldn't happen. The doctors failed. The laws failed. The police failed. They let us down, and I hate them all!"*

Another form anger takes is rage at the disease, the drugs, the addiction, the virus. "AIDS has screwed up our lives," says Mark. "It's robbed us of everything we took so long to build." AIDS only compounds our feelings of powerlessness, our sense that life is unmanageable and out of control. We wonder, *Why did this damned disease have to enter our lives—my life?*

Add to this our anger at friends and family. Here we directly confront society's fears and the stigma toward people with AIDS. We can find ourselves asking, "Where are our so-called friends now? . . . Why does our family avoid us? . . . Why doesn't anyone call or write anymore?" This is the pain felt by Charlie and Millie relating to their children.

At this point it's easy to feel abandoned, betrayed. In moments of self-pity we watch the thought arise, *Our friends didn't really care for us. Was it all a sham?* And even though we're not truly alone, we feel that way. Mark feels such isolation in watching others' reactions. "When friends ask how my Dan is doing, I don't tell them because I know they really don't want to hear it. I feel them squirm when I cry, so I keep it to myself."

When this feeling runs deep enough, caregivers can anticipate rejection. Sometimes, to avoid rejection, we withdraw and isolate ourselves. Fearing abandonment, we reject our friends and families first, often acting out in an angry way: "Leave me alone. Leave us alone. Don't help me. I don't need you or anyone." The pain behind such anger can be overwhelming.

Anger can cut deep into spirituality, surfacing as anger at God. One person may turn to traditional religion and find no response to this anger. Another person, who is spiritual in a non-traditional way, may discover a similar void. In either case, the anger may lead to doubt and despair. And for those of us in Twelve Step programs, such anger can hinder our spirituality: prayer, meditation, and "conscious contact" with our Higher Power. Yolanda continually thinks, *Why is this happening to us? Why me? What kind of world is this? How could God let this go on? Where is my faith when I need it now? I turn to my religion, and there's nothing there for me. I'm alone and help- less. There's no help anywhere. It's not fair. I don't deserve this. Car- men doesn't deserve this.*

To our surprise—and sometimes our shame—there's also anger toward the person with AIDS, the person we're caring for. "How could he let this happen?" Mark asks. "Didn't Dan know what would happen? How could he do this to me? How could he be so stupid? Why did I ever get involved with him? I want to live and have fun; he just wants to sleep. After all this, he's just going to leave me and I'll be alone." In the midst of it, we ask how we can possibly be angry at someone who's sick, someone we love, someone who may die.

Finally, there's the movement of anger building on itself. Though powerful, this anger about one's own anger often eludes our awareness. "I just feel angry all the time," Millie reports without knowing why. "I'm angry at everybody and nobody. I snap at waitresses and co-workers about nothing. Why do I get like this? I get so fed up with my own behavior."

We may turn that anger inward, accusing ourselves of feel- ing impatient, of being selfish, of not being good enough. And in this anger we discover roots of other feelings: sad- ness, shame, guilt, and anxiety.

Sadness

As caregivers, we feel grief, loss, and sadness. Our sadness has these subtle dimensions, centering on loss that's real or imagined. Projecting loss—something that's well known to alcoholics and their loved ones—is also common in those who love someone with AIDS.

What kinds of loss are we speaking of here? They include lost dreams and a lost future. "We had so much going for us," Mark says, tears burning his cheeks. "Things were going right for us. Now we're losing all of it. All the things we looked forward to—all the projects, the vacations, the good times—there's no chance of them now."

Millie describes her sadness over the lost present: "There's so much I want to do today, but there will be no time for any of it. How will I make it through today? We're so busy with this disease, we really aren't loving each other or having any fun. No kids, no friends, no more money—it's too much!"

And Inez asks, "Why do I have to worry about Mom being sick? I just want to play with the other kids."

Lost pleasures, lost sex, and the loss of love—each of these mires us in sadness. "This will put an end to our sex life," Mark concludes. "It was so comforting, so good. Will the other things we enjoyed be taken from us too? Sometimes we don't even feel like a couple anymore. Dan's a patient. He's distant. He's a person who needs to be cared for. And me, I'm the nurse. We're not lovers now; we can't be. I miss the good old days."

Lost health is a factor too. "Charlie is sick, getting sicker. That causes me a lot of pain. It's starting to get to me too," Millie says. "I get colds more often, flus more often. I just feel tired all the time. I can't remember the last time I really felt good. With his every cough, his every pain, I ache inside."

What often hits hardest at first is loss of friends and family relationships. "I feel like we're outcasts now, like lepers," says Millie. "We're alone. I miss them. I ache for Charlene and her daughter. I can't tell them how I really feel. I don't want to burden them—they can't help anyway. They don't want to know."

Loss of certainty and loss of routine, though more subtle, can be just as troublesome. It's natural to feel, as Mark admitted, that "things are all messed up now." He says, "I never know what's happening. The days are all wrong, and I'm never in control of my time anymore. I don't know what will happen next. I'm not even sure what's happening right now. He may be fine one day, sick or in the hospital the next. How can we plan a vacation, a concert, a dinner with friends?"

Then there's the loss of intimacy caused by keeping secrets: *Who do I tell?* wonders Millie. *Who can we trust? We can't really tell anyone about AIDS — even our friends. They won't really know what's going on. I won't feel close to them anymore.* At Charlie's birthday dinner, Millie's heart was breaking. She thought, *How can I tell Charlie how I really feel? He has enough problems. I don't want to add to them.*

Still another element of sadness is pity for the person with AIDS. That person can look so sick, helpless, and frail. "I just wanted to hold Carmen in my arms and rock her like a baby," says Yolanda. "If only I could wave a wand and make it all go away. But I can't. I cry myself to sleep every night."

A closely related brand of sadness is self-pity. We can easily wonder why this has to happen to us — especially at this time in our life. As caregivers, we can feel so alone, so scared, so small. Inez says it for all of us: "Can't someone just take care of me and make it all go away?"

It is common that when the disease progresses, our feelings progress as well. Sadness turns into despair for many of us as things get worse, and we lose hope. Despair and hopelessness may lead to thoughts of suicide — a normal response to such feelings. Out of despair comes the inclination to give up. If we feel truly hopeless about the situation, the thought arises, *Why go on? I don't want to live like this. It's not worth it. Why go through what I've seen others go through?* Mark thought to himself, *If Dan dies, I can't go on.* Each day Millie feels, *It isn't worth it anymore. And what's left? Just misery day in and day out.*

For many people, fatalism is their response to hopelessness. Some even start to self-destruct. They start using again, and their hard-won sobriety is lost. They practice unsafe sex. Or they're seized by compulsive behavior: overeating, oversleeping, overworking.

Woven into the anger and sadness are two closely related feelings: shame and guilt.

Shame and Guilt

Caregivers talk about feeling both shame and guilt. Stated simply, shame is a belief that there's something intrinsically wrong with us as people. Deep inside, we feel fundamentally flawed. We feel we are defective, and others can tell. With shame, writes therapist Mic Hunter, we feel "someone has seen our real self and we're sure they're disgusted."[2]

Shame is compounded by several factors. One is the stark fact that AIDS is a stigmatized disease, much like cancer and tuberculosis once were. It's the unspeakable "A" word—one that many people would rather not mention in polite conversation. And if the person with AIDS or the caregiver is gay, chances are they're already carrying a truckload of shame. *I'm bad already. Something is wrong with me; something has always been wrong with me. My essence is bad. And this just adds to it.* In a similar way, shame might arise over being an alcoholic, an other drug addict, a woman, an African American, a Hispanic, or a member of another minority group.

Though many people confuse guilt and shame, guilt is a feeling with different dynamics. Melody Beattie, author of *Beyond Codependency: And Getting Better All the Time*, explains it this way:

> Guilt is believing that what we did isn't okay. Authentic guilt is valuable. It's a signal that we've violated our own, or a universal, moral code. It helps keep us honest, healthy, and on track. Shame is worthless. Shame is the belief that whether what we did is okay or not, who we are isn't.[3]

According to Claudia Black, author of *It Will Never Happen to Me!*, guilt is an "internal feeling of regret and responsibility for actions that violate a personal standard."[4] As such, guilt is specifically related to an action or an event. Dr. Black also distinguishes "false guilt," a sense of responsibility for things that go wrong—things for which we are not responsible.

False guilt might surface first in a conviction of "failure." "I was a bad parent, a lousy lover," Millie convinces herself. "I got angry too much. I was never patient enough, never good enough. I'm still not good enough, not strong enough to handle all this. I don't know how to help my husband. I'm just no good. It's my fault."

Self-blame is at work here too. We often ask these questions about the people we're caring for: "Why did she go on drugs? . . . Why did he become gay? . . . Why did he get the virus?" Soon this search for a culprit turns on us.

Mark says, "What if I caused Dan's sickness? It's all my fault. After all, I've been exposed to the virus too. In the past, I've practiced unsafe sex despite knowing better, especially when drunk or stoned."

Carmen's mother says, "If I had done my job, none of this would have happened. My daughter went wrong because I didn't spend enough time raising her. We didn't have enough money to buy her things — clothes, toys. That's why she ran away at age fifteen. I'm worthless as a parent."

"Our marriage was loveless because of me. I'm not a good lover. It was my fault if he got involved with someone else and got the virus," Millie says to herself again and again — even though Charlie denied sleeping with anyone but Millie in their twenty-five years together. "I expected too much; I was too selfish. He feels alone, and if he keeps drinking, it will be my fault too!"

Inez believes that "if Mama dies, it will be my fault. She's sick because I was a bad girl."

"Sometimes I even wish he would just die and get it over with. How could I feel that?" asked Mark in a therapy session, feeling more guilty than ever.

What can be crushing about shame or self-blame is the weight of obligation. In speaking about this, we recite our list of "shoulds":

- "I should have been more caring and more patient when he was well."
- "I should have been a better lover to her."
- "I never gave enough; I should have given more."
- "I never did enough, communicated enough."
- "I should have let him do more of what he wanted, talked more, listened more, cared more."

Through all this, shame creates uncertainty. It's not only *what did I do to cause this?* It's also *will I fail again in the future? . . . Will I be any good at what's to come? . . . What if I end up alone? . . . What if she gets sicker? . . . Will I let them put her on a respirator?* For Mark, the internal dialogue went much like this: *If he goes back on AZT, he can't use the new experimental drug, the one that sounds so good. I just don't know. And I should know, after all. He may die if I don't make the right choice. I'm responsible.*

In short, we wonder about doing the right thing, about knowing when to keep trying and when to let go. Again, false guilt is at work here—a sense of taking on responsibility for another person's well-being. We feel guilty about our lack of power. By ourselves, we cannot cure AIDS. We forget the simple fact that *no one can,* not even the experts. That feeling —we should do more even though we can't—is a hallmark of codependence.

Anxiety

Caregivers commonly feel anxiety. We wake with it and go to sleep with it; we live with it for days, for weeks at a time.

What is anxiety? It's something more powerful than an isolated fear. Instead, it is a tightness, a cramping, a gripping fear that crawls into every corner of life. Sometimes the very experience of being afraid makes us even more afraid. Afraid of what? Often we can't say.

This overwhelming blend of fear and uncertainty is anxiety.

The phrase *fear of the unknown* describes it. Will the person with AIDS live for ten days, ten months, or ten years? We don't know. In that vacuum of knowledge, it's easy to project into the future. We picture the worst that can happen, running a painful scenario in our minds and our dreams. Yolanda voices her fear in a support group: "Every time Carmen gets sick, I worry that it's another bout of pneumonia, and this time I know it will be worse." That kind of negative rehearsal and projection generates anxiety.

Beyond this, anxiety is a vague, free-floating nervousness that's hard to pin down: "I'm nervous all the time, and I don't know why. I'm not sure what I fear." Since anxiety is central to our journey, we'll come back to it several times in later chapters.

Shock

Caregivers commonly experience shock when finding out their friend or loved one has AIDS. We saw this clearly with Mark, Millie, and Carmen's families. Like anxiety, shock will be a theme woven throughout this book. Shock naturally occurs with the initial, overwhelming experience of discovery and diagnosis. But it also recurs over time — for example, if a loved one's condition worsens or changes.

Shock is typically the first emotion, a visceral, gut response. There's nothing intellectual about it: People faint; they turn pale and their eyes widen; they're unable to comprehend the doctor's words; the message just doesn't register. This is quite in keeping with the dictionary definition of *shock*, "a disturbance of equilibrium."[5]

Denial

With that disturbance comes denial, disbelief, or a refusal to believe. Millie protests, "There's been a mistake. Say it again."

"You don't really mean that, do you?" yells Mark. "It can't be!"

We may act out our denial. We insist on repeating the HIV antibody test again and again, far beyond the point that it's useful, hoping for a negative result. Or we switch from doctor to doctor, specialist to specialist, each time hoping we'll find an expert to magically erase the test results.

This denial may represent our profound resistance to acknowledging the new reality. In fact, this is one of the ways we defend ourselves against pain: We cling to the status quo. We pretend that nothing has really changed, that the scenery is still the same. Until the diagnosis, Mark never had to say the words "Dan has AIDS, and I am his caregiver." Now this simple sentence underscores the radical change in his life. Early on, denial is saying "everything's fine" and believing it, even as life begins to crumble around us.

Withdrawal

Closely linked to denial is withdrawal. There's a universal desire to want to run away from the truth, from the intense feelings that are involved, from people. Charlie, for example, shuts down when he hears the diagnosis. He walks away to avoid hearing anymore. Withdrawing even further, he gets drunk. And inside, he dies a little, numbing himself to the truth of his diagnosis.

But withdrawal doesn't have to be this obvious; it can take more subtle forms as well. Withdrawal can be as simple and unnoticed as changing the subject whenever AIDS comes up. It can mean shutting out any conversation about AIDS. It can mean refusing to read the latest article on AIDS, or changing channels when AIDS makes the TV news. Withdrawal can also be more than outwardly walking away from the persons we care for. It can be an inner movement of the soul, a contraction of the heart as well. Withdrawal is alienation from others, from oneself, and often from God.

Rehashing the Past

With the diagnosis of AIDS comes an inevitable question for the person with AIDS. We hear it in Charlie's words: "Why? How did this happen? Who gave it to me? Where did I get it?" At the same time, Millie as caregiver is also asking why: "Why is this happening? What did *I* do? Was I a part of this? Could I have done something differently to avoid this?" For some of us, this is the first step in an endless round of justification, blame, and rehashing the past.

Millie, for example, rehashes the events leading up to Charlie's diagnosis of AIDS. She rehearses those events again and again. Each time the result is the same; she gets stuck. No real insights emerge. Instead, she's mired in an endless list of "if onlys": "If only Charlie hadn't had that unit of blood. . . . If only we'd changed doctors. . . . If only I hadn't urged him to get the surgery. . . . If only I'd taken him to Mayo Clinic instead of that hospital. . . . If only I had donated blood. . . . If only I knew more about this, I would have suspected. . . . If only, if only . . ." And then comes another round of false guilt for Millie to heap on herself.

Blame

One desperate, quick "fix" for the emotions generated by the diagnosis of AIDS is blame. In blaming, people find a scapegoat. They grope for a way to sidestep any sense of responsibility. Carmen's family and Dan's family can blame their loved one's behavior: "You did drugs. You were promiscuous. You went out of the relationship and screwed someone. That's what caused this." Millie can't do that, so she blames the doctors and the hospital. Then she blames herself in true codependent fashion. At one point she suspects Charlie of having had an affair, but then she again blames herself for not being a better wife and lover. And she will not voice any of this to Charlie.

In each case, our capacity to blame can be limitless. This tactic perpetuates itself; blame begets more blame. With it, we stay chained to the wheel of negative emotions.

Piling Reaction on Top of Reaction

In this chapter we've created an inventory of the feelings that may occur in Stage One. Yet even the most exhaustive list of emotions will be only one-dimensional, for these feelings are moving on many levels. Not only do caregivers react to the diagnosis of AIDS, *we react to the way others react.*

- Seeing Dan's shock and sadness at the diagnosis only ignites more anger and fear for Mark.
- Millie, sensing that Charlie has simply decided to be a victim, is drawn even deeper into despair.
- Inez, seeing Yolanda and Carmen argue, develops severe headaches as her fear of abandonment accelerates.

Moving through Stage One calls on us first to become aware of this complex fabric of feelings. If we don't, our feelings may escalate while a healing response eludes us.

SHARING INFORMATION: WHO HAS THE RIGHT TO KNOW?

During Stage One, many of us feel the need to tell someone that our loved one has AIDS. And immediately this imposes a double bind. To move beyond our Stage One feelings, it helps to share them with someone. In many cases, being open and honest is simply a practical necessity. For instance, we may want to talk to lawyers and have a will made. And protecting the people we've been sexual with may mean telling them too.

But suppose we decide to tell some people. What happens

if they, in turn, tell others? And do we dare to talk about AIDS in a Twelve Step meeting or any other support group? For Mark, Millie, and Carmen's family, the question about who to tell comes up again and again. In some cases, it's a source of endless tension, and it never truly gets resolved. Dan and Charlie, for example, don't want to tell anyone about their diagnosis of AIDS, and this strains their relationships with Mark and Millie. Carmen's illness is common knowledge in the neighborhood, even though Hermenia wishes it wasn't.

The core issue here is whose information is this? Who has the right to tell? The person with AIDS? The caregiver? Both? Again, even this decision may be taken from us; AIDS may reveal itself. There may be no secrecy if the person we care for is sick, young, addicted to drugs, or gay. If that person enters the hospital with pneumonia, AIDS may be suspected immediately.

The decision about whom to tell is a milestone in the journey of AIDS caregivers. In fact, it signals a change from Stage One, discovery, to the next stage, adapting. When we come to grips with how to share this information, we're really setting the pattern for how we intend to live the rest of our life with the fact of AIDS. And as we'll see in the next chapter, sharing information is only one of the tasks we'll face.

CHAPTER 4

Stage Two: Adapting—
Building a New Life

Millie set the table like a Vegas sharpie dealing cards. For months she had worked herself into a domestic frenzy: cleaning the attic, painting the basement, scrubbing the kitchen walls. It was the only way she knew how to release anger and frustration. She wouldn't dream of "battling it out" with Charlie, who was now working half time. She always tried to put on a smile for him.

Charlie was growing insular, languid, bitter, and miserable. It was very difficult for Charlie to be helpless and dependent. The disease, the night sweats, the fatigue, the pain in his legs, the fever and the depression—all of it made him helpless and dependent. Despite Millie's urging him to go to meetings, he stopped attending his noon "stag meeting"— the AA group for men, which always gave him a lift. Instead, he came home to sleep. He'd get up to eat supper, watch TV, and then go back to sleep. Loss of energy and loss of income were secondary to the loss of his good relationship with his daughter and grandchild. The new baby was due in three weeks, and he had not seen his daughter or granddaughter in four months. It broke his heart.

He cursed Odell, his son-in-law. The few phone conversations they had always ended in him threatening Odell.

Millie would attempt to calm Charlie down, knowing that stress was not good for the immune system.

"I knew Odell was a simpleton the first time I laid eyes on him," said Charlie. He often said, even before his diagnosis and Odell's decision to ostracize the family, "Odell is so narrow-minded. If he fell on a pin, it would blind him in both eyes." Despite Millie's intervention; despite her sending pamphlets about AIDS; despite a letter from Dr. Maiman to Odell and Charlene assuring them that Charlene's pregnancy would not be affected by her father's HIV status, nor would their daughter's well-being be affected by a grandfather with AIDS; despite all of it, they chose to stay away.

And Millie refused to go to her daughter, son-in-law, and grandchild for a visit. "If you shut out Daddy, Charlene, you can't have me."

"I'm not shutting him out of my life, Mama," protested Charlene. "I'm only doing it for the health of his unborn grandchild. And besides, I told you I'd be happy to call him every day, but he won't talk to me."

With Charlie refusing to discuss his illness or permitting his wife to tell anyone, Millie's stress level increased. She finally bit the bullet and went for her own HIV antibody test. Much to her relief, it was negative. She had hardly been sexual with Charlie for years.

Part of her wanted to tell her friends about Charlie's illness, mostly Al-Anon people she'd grown to trust over the years. Another part of her saw the ostracism that was occurring within her own nuclear family. "If our own flesh and blood is treating us this way, I can imagine how others will react." But the pressure got to be too intense, and after four months, she began attending AIDS caregiver support groups. Millie learned she had to take care of herself so she could take care of her ailing husband.

With this in mind, Millie made a momentous decision: She secretly told Brenda, her sister-in-law and best friend, about Charlie's illness. It was a relief for her to unload, to unburden herself to her confidante. But it was also painful. She felt she'd betrayed and deceived Charlie. She'd been through a lot during the years Charlie drank, and she was able to handle it all. But AIDS renewed her worries about the alcohol slips she knew he'd been having. Now, she needed help.

* * * * *

At first Dan and Mark were depressed. Almost weekly they received calls from friends in New York City, Chicago, Los Angeles, and San Francisco, informing them of some acquaintance or buddy's death due to AIDS. Mark was becoming more and more depressed with widowerhood looming. His spirits sagged.

He was not permitted to share the secret. The only person to whom he could "vent" was his friend Pepper, whom he'd told about Dan's diagnosis even before he told Dan that weekend in Ocean Beach. But Pepper was often not available or unwilling to listen. She grew distant, remote.

Mark was reluctant to talk about these unpleasant feelings with Dan. Such conversations always led to tears, and it saddened Dan to see Mark weep. It was Dan's modus operandi to change the subject to anything—Khmerian cuisine, Ryukyuan circumcision, monkeys at the zoo—or to quickly suggest an impromptu outing, party, or some frivolous diversion. Anything but AIDS. Rarely did Dan cry, and he never cried out of self-pity. He cried when he thought of Mark's sorrow and Mark's tears. Dan shed tears because of babies and toddlers with AIDS too. The thought of these little ones being so wickedly snuffed out was more than even Dan could bear.

But the months of secret-keeping were getting to Mark, and his resentment and anger were building. He was determined to have his way, to make Dan come out of the closet with regard to his illness. It would be a tough job and Dan would resist, but wasn't the Hellespont spanned, wasn't Mount Everest conquered?

Dan continued to remind Mark what their "shrink" had told them when they first found out about the diagnosis: It's Dan's illness. Illness is personal, and disclosure should come at his own pace. Under no circumstances should Dan buckle under to Mark's persistent pleas to tell their friends and relatives. But Dan knew Mark's great need to share, to be totally honest, and Dan's resistance to sharing the secret was slowly, laboriously eroded. They decided to tell their best friends in Phoenix, Evin and Cal. Even then, Dan had his doubts. "Why do I feel like some innocent and trusting sheep being led through Swift and Company's little green door?" he asked.

Within the next month, and with Dan's reluctant permission, Mark and Dan told four people of particular importance to Mark: Mark's AA sponsor in Phoenix; Sherman, Mark's old college roommate and now their friend; an elderly therapist couple—neighbors, actually—who became confidants and friends in Boston; and Ellen and her husband, David. Disclosure to Ellen was especially important to Mark. He looked upon her, this best friend of his, as Earth Mother. His opinion of her could not be overstated.

Dan thought that telling these people should suffice and give Mark the support system he needed. But within weeks, Mark came up with five or six more people, "good friends" he thought should know. "I feel so deceitful when they ask me what's new or how our health is," complained Mark.

In the meantime, Dan continued to draw a distinction between denial and privacy. His disease was a private concern. He felt awkward and uncomfortable showing eight-by-tens of his personal life. "I'm not having open house on my soul this week," he'd say. Yet he and Mark knew full well that the disease was there: the horrible fatigue, a few new lesions, slight loss of memory, and frequent train of thought derailment.

Dan took treatments—AZT—which caused terrible anemia and was soon discontinued. He and Mark wrote wills, checked life insurance and health coverage, and took part in some experimental protocols for new medications. There were monthly blood tests, monthly checkups, monthly visits to doctors. Dan, who'd pass out at the sight of a rare steak, grew inured to all these medical procedures and doctors' appointments.

Mark would push the boundaries even further regarding sharing the secret. Twice weekly, he'd attempt to get Dan into AIDS support groups or to get him to tell his mother, Phyllis, that he was sick. The conversations would always begin, "Dan, here's something to think about, just a thought." Dan had all the food for thought he could stomach and insisted enough was enough. The thought of Phyllis finding out that he had AIDS made him sick to his stomach. He feared endless lecturing if not outright rejection.

Aside from that major issue—sharing the secret—there were no crisis issues. Mark saw his raison d'être as ministering to Dan and making sure Dan got everything and anything he ever wanted. Dan was pampered. Acquaintances would say he was spoiled. He corrected them and said he was spared, and he knew Mark was delighted to "go the extra mile" for him.

The men made a decision to spend money, to be frivolous. They adopted a new spending philosophy, asking themselves three questions before making any purchase: "Do we really need it? Can we really afford it? Why not get it anyway?" They also became sybarites, opting for the maximum pleasure in life. And to further this end they decided that Dan should quit his job and seek part-time employment. Clearly, this would give Dan time to do the things he ordinarily could not do had he been working full time, and it would also help the healing process.

Dan's disease certainly brought the two men closer

together. It made Dan really appreciate Mark, and it made Mark appreciate the time he had left with Dan.

* * * * *

Carmen was on the phone to Hermenia making arrangements to be picked up at the hospital. She was excited because she was being released from the hospital the next day. Since her diagnosis fourteen months earlier, she had been in and out of the hospital four times. She had given up her apartment, gone on disability, gotten back together and broken up with Xavier twice, relapsed and gotten clean and sober twice. To date, she had four months of uneasy sobriety.

Although she was glad to be leaving the hospital, she was dreading going back to the apartment she now shared with her mother, Inez, and little Xavier. The one bedroom apartment, located in Spanish Harlem.

The only other option she had was to patch things up with Xavier and go back to their old apartment two blocks away. She knew Yolanda, Hermenia, and Inez would not take well to such a decision. She and they knew going back to Xavier meant going back to drugs, to careless morals, and to questionable friends. Yolanda, especially, would not approve.

No, *thought Carmen,* going back to Xavier is out of the question. I'll go back to Mama's apartment and make the best of it. Besides, I'll be attending a lot of NA meetings and AIDS support group meetings. *She was well liked and even loved in those groups.* I'll even volunteer to speak, if Mama lets me, *thought Carmen.*

Hermenia was having a very difficult time adjusting to her daughter's disease. Neighbors whispered. It was embarrassing for Hermenia. Having a daughter who had AIDS meant having a daughter who was a tramp, a drug addict. She was evasive when friends inquired about Carmen. But an even bigger source of distress and depression to Carmen was her concern about little Xavier, who had been born HIV positive. Thank God there were no outward signs of the disease yet.

Carmen heard Yolanda walking down the hospital corridor to the ward. Carmen said good-bye to Hermenia as Yolanda entered the room. She brought Carmen a used book, the perennial best-seller by Adelle Davis, Let's Eat Right to Keep Fit.

Yolanda began lecturing Carmen about building up her strength and resistance through good food. She knew that her cousin was not a good cook. When Carmen, Xavier, and the children were living as a family, suppers were improvised from tins. Yolanda used to visit the apartment regularly to prepare hot meals because the whole family looked thin. She suspected that if she did not intervene, their destinies would be dark and tragic. Once again Yolanda was prepared to fatten Carmen up and lead her on the path of nutrition and well being. She also brought glad tidings from Carmen's NA friends.

For the next few months, Carmen attended various AIDS support groups three or four times a week. She did this despite Hermenia's strong objections, but with Yolanda's encouragement. Carmen was recognized as pert, sassy, outspoken, and honest. She was asked to speak at several high schools about the dangers of drugs. "Now everyone will know," complained Hermenia.

The only time Carmen thought of death was when she was in the hospital; otherwise she enjoyed her new popularity as a tell-it-all, let-it-all-hang-out speaker. There were days when her "performances" were not up to snuff and days when her appearances had to be cancelled because of fatigue. On days like this, especially, she counted on Inez's and Yolanda's help with little Xavier, grocery shopping, and housecleaning.

Inez, who'd been skipping school to help care for little Xavier, looked at the pile of dirty clothes and diapers. She had to do the laundry today and prepare dinner. Childhood play was not part of Inez's life because of adult responsibilities. But Inez didn't seem to mind. She enjoyed helping nurse her mother back to health, and she enjoyed caring for her little brother. But the burden placed on her young shoulders worsened her headaches. Although she knew she could do no more for them, she worried about Mom's health and sobriety, and the health of little Xavier.

Yolanda often lamented to herself that she had no life of her own, aside from helping and being there for Carmen. But she was always there, always offering advice, always helping. Carmen truly became the focus of her existence. Only rarely did she allow the thought to enter her awareness, God help me. What will I do when she dies?

* * * * *

THE TASKS OF ADAPTING

Adapting is what we do to try and make life regular again. Mark described it as being like "diving into freezing water. I shiver. I get goose pimples. I start flailing my arms and legs. I do anything to get my body temperature back to normal and lessen the chill." This analogy is about establishing a new equilibrium, and it describes Stage Two.

Stage Two involves a series of responses with one aim: relieving the discomfort we described in Stage One. After all, no one could live each day with the full intensity of Stage One feelings. We must do something to get on with our life.

And what can we do? Adapting is a task that reverberates on many levels of the self. There are at least three levels involved in Stage Two.

First, there's the level of the intellect, the thinking mind. This means grappling with new questions:

- "What's the plan of treatment for my loved one with AIDS?"

- "As a caregiver, what are my life plans?"
- "What are our plans for being together? Can we even *make* plans?"

Coming to grips with such questions is at the heart of Stage Two. And at this level, people do "head stuff": they plan, reason, weigh alternatives, consider consequences, and seek answers.

A second Stage Two task goes directly to the heart. It involves the way people "carry" their pain. This is an issue for many people besides the primary caregiver and the person newly diagnosed with AIDS. It spreads in ever-widening circles. Parents, friends, children, partners, spouses — we all change in response to AIDS. We have to. And all of us may feel the emotional pain.

During Stage Two, the way we choose to adapt will determine our experience of pain. Even in the face of chronic illness, some of us are able to decrease or "turn down" the pain. We cannot erase the intrusive event — the diagnosis. Even so, we can *feel* the pain with less intensity. By adjusting our internal responses — our thoughts and feelings — we can modify our response to AIDS. And that leads to a different *experience* of pain.

Even in the realm of feeling, we can speak of certain responses as pain "amplifiers," pain "reducers," or pain "relievers." Evidence for this comes with Mark, Millie, and Yolanda as they move through Stage Two.

- Mark relieves pain by talking to friends and attending support groups.
- Yolanda seeks to reduce the pain in her family by cooking, caring for the household, attending to Inez, and focusing on Carmen.
- In contrast, Millie attempts to numb feeling. She keeps busy — she cleans, paints, and scrubs — and in that frenzy, she prays for distraction from her pain. This has the potential to amplify the pain she'll feel in later stages.

Besides changing our response to pain and asking questions, we have a third major Stage Two task—taking action. We do whatever we can to change our environment, the real circumstances of our life. This covers a whole range of behaviors. Examples are as varied as we are: cutting back to part-time work, moving to a new city, joining a support group, finding a new doctor, seeking out new friends.

All these actions have one aim: to make things "normal" again, to make things somehow "right," to establish a new routine. Only this time, the routine must be built on a new reality—life with AIDS. Sometimes it feels like the day after Hiroshima, that our world will never go back to the way it was. In light of this, things can hardly be normal again. Rather, they must be *normalized,* somehow made regular in the midst of turbulent and permanent change.

STYLES OF ADAPTING

So people adapt to AIDS in three basic ways: thinking, changing their emotional responses, and taking action. To carry out these tasks, however, people use a number of different strategies. Taken together, those strategies make up a highly personal way of building a new life and forging a new identity. Thus, we can accurately speak of Stage Two "styles."

It's important to note that some strategies work better than others. That is, some coping strategies lead to less pain, less grief, less sadness, less shame overall. These responses may even breathe an air of serenity and acceptance into our life. Other strategies, however, work for some people but not others. And some strategies can spiral us downward into deeper cycles of pain, tension, and loss.

In Part Three, we'll talk more about the "healing" and "hurting" aspects of our coping strategies. That is, some strategies promote our mental and physical health; others undermine us. For now, we'll simply list some strategies without evaluating them in detail.

Denial

At one end of the spectrum, denial hurts us. How? By helping us to run from the truth, to deny the fact that our loved one has AIDS. In effect, this forces people to stay stuck with Stage One feelings such as anger, shock, shame, sadness, and grief. This only delays us from moving on.

There is another side to denial, however. We call it *positive denial.* That involves viewing our life with some perspective, some detachment—even some humor. While fully admitting that AIDS has entered our life, we can choose to think about other things instead. At some moments, even such benign denial will not be appropriate. At other times, we can laugh, making light of the situation and puncturing the constant seriousness.

Mark uses positive denial, and says, "Yes, AIDS is a fact in our lives. But we don't need to think about it all the time. We can even talk about *not talking* about AIDS. When a negative thought or feeling comes up, Dan and I can be fully aware of it and still choose to move away from it." Doing so bypasses fear, sadness, and negative projections into the future—a dead end.

This contrasts with the full denial by Hermenia. Despite the fact that Carmen was out lecturing about AIDS, in Hermenia's household the word *AIDS* is never spoken; there the women only mouth the word without uttering a sound.

The Mental Review

One of the central tasks we face as AIDS caregivers sounds absurdly simple: merely remembering the fact that a person we love has AIDS. Yet, if the forces of denial in us are strong, we may need to consciously remind ourselves—again and again—that life has truly changed. This does not have to be elaborate; it can be as simple as waking up and doing a one minute "mental review." All that may be needed is an acknowledgment. Millie can say, "Charlie has AIDS. I am his caregiver. Yes, our lives have changed forever. So now it's time to get up and make breakfast." Again, this is part of adapting. Even if things cannot really be normal, they can be normalized—made *like* normal.

Grieving

Part of adapting is grieving. People grieve in their own ways. For Mark, grief is something that rises easily to the surface. He embraces Dan and cries; there's no need, he says, to "stuff" these feelings. Beyond this, Mark will go to other people and cry with them. He'll also cry at night, alone. Dan, on the other hand, does not cry much at all. Still, for him there is no sense of denying grief. He simply wears his grief differently. He experiences it privately. "After all," he says, "why talk about it all the time?"

Charlie doggedly refuses to give his grief any quarter. He sits like a statue, stuffs feelings, and sinks into despair, like slowly suffocating in quicksand. This response creates his individual experience of pain. Millie works to swallow her feelings, especially when she's with Charlie. Since no one offers support, she cries alone until she tells her sister-in-law, Brenda.

Carmen embodies yet another style. For her, grief arises as frenetic action. Her style is impulsive and explosive. One day she announces plans to go to ninety Narcotics Anonymous meetings in ninety days; then within twenty-four hours, she wants to use drugs or see Xavier.

Making Decisions

After the diagnosis of AIDS starts to sink in, a host of practical questions arise. "Shall we make funeral plans? . . .

What about wills? . . . Do we need to change our insurance policies? . . . How will my career be affected? . . . Who will have durable power of attorney — control over life-and-death decisions — if my loved one is incapacitated?"

Underlying all these pragmatic concerns, however, is a more philosophical one: "What do I want to do the rest of my life? I've just learned that your life span is limited; now, how do we respond in daily life?" Making decisions about these questions will help reduce our anxiety and fear. As such, these decisions are the core of adapting.

Seizing the Present

When confronted with the possibility of a shortened life span, some people with AIDS and their caregivers make a conscious decision to make the most of the present. Their guiding principle, in effect, becomes, *Why postpone joy?* This is the preferred style for Dan and Mark. They adapt by working less, looking for other sources of money, and changing their style of investing. Though they still save, the future is really short-term, and one that doesn't include retirement. So Dan and Mark focus more on the here and now. They travel, go to shows, and enjoy eating out. And even though they wonder if it will ever happen, they plan a vacation for next year.

Hopelessness and Thoughts of Suicide

We mentioned suicidal thoughts as part of Stage One. It's important to note that such thoughts may recur in later stages as well. Moreover, they may come to both the person with AIDS and the caregiver.

In Stage Two, suicidal thoughts may have a "practical" tinge. At this point, some people with AIDS and their caregivers talk of suicide pacts. Even Millie thinks through some of the possible consequences: *If Charlie kills himself, our life insurance may not pay off. What can we do about this?* . . .

What if I commit suicide? But when? Now? When the pain starts? Later? . . . What if things get better? . . . Can Charlie bear to be without me? Can I bear to be without him? Here, practical questions mix with explosive feelings.

Acting-Out

Acting-out is another Stage One behavior that may carry over into the adapting stage. Again, it involves blunting pain through high-risk or addictive behaviors: unsafe sex, using alcohol or other drugs, overeating, and similar behaviors. Such behaviors often lead to more difficulty in adapting.

Talking About Relationships

Before AIDS, we may not have talked much about relationship issues with the person we care for. Now, relationship issues may become a central concern. And for good reason. In Stage Two, relationships can assume totally new directions. People with AIDS and their caregivers may grow closer. They may grow apart. Their relationships may drift without commitment. Relationships may end, or they may assume entirely new forms. Lovers may become friends; children, like Inez, may act as parents.

The basic questions are these:

- "Do we talk about the new shape of our lives? Do we talk more openly about things?"
- "How do we deal with the shame and the blame?"
- "We've been through shock, a roller coaster of emotion; now what do we do about those feelings?"
- "Will AIDS end our relationship or deepen it?"

The vow to remain together "until death do us part" suddenly assumes a new significance.

At this point, caregivers often wonder about breaking away from the person with AIDS. In fact, it's common for chronic illness of any type to strain relationships or end them. Millie, for instance, thinks about leaving Charlie: *Maybe I don't have to live with this.* The stigma associated with AIDS can also prompt resignation. Millie thinks: *I bet Charlie was out with a whore, and that's how he got AIDS. I should just leave him. But how could I leave him now? He's so sick, so weak, so helpless.* She feels trapped, so she stays.

To move through Stage Two, it helps to ask how committed we are to the relationship. We can ask ourselves, "Do I want to stay with the person I care for? Could this relationship change or end?" Our answers are so important that they will govern the rest of our caregiving journey.

For many of us, as for Mark and Millie, sex has much to do with these questions. The questions are these:

- "Can we be sexual with each other?"
- "Can we practice safer sex?"
- "What does that take from the experience?"
- "And is safer sex really safe?"

Sexual desire varies in this new light. For Charlie and Millie, it disappears. It died, in fact, before AIDS.

For Carmen, sexual desire rises. "I haven't got much time left," she protests. "I'm empty, and I need someone to love. I still deserve to be happy and fulfilled."

For Dan, on the other hand, sexual desire shuts down. This forces hard questions on Mark: "Do I look elsewhere for sex and subject myself to danger? Am I able to practice safer sex?"

People with AIDS and their caregivers often confront these questions without any clear guidelines or role models. This only reinforces a fact about adapting: how we move through this stage is based on individual needs and choices.

Deciding on Treatment

There are hundreds of possible treatments for AIDS. Traditional medical options include AZT, pentamidine, repeat testing, and follow-up visits to a primary doctor or specialist. Side by side with these exists a panoply of experimental and non-traditional treatments: everything from macrobiotics and AL 721 (an egg protein thought to have antiviral properties), to buyer's clubs (organized groups that share access to new and unapproved treatments for AIDS), placebos, and experimental trials of new drugs like Peptide T and DDI.

The questions become:

- "Whom do we believe?"
- "Shall we combine traditional and experimental treatments?"
- "How do we choose one over the other?"
- "And how do we all cope with side-effects?"

Here, again, we face uncertainty. And while the answers we find are tentative, any treatment we do choose may lock us into a rigid course for a lifetime. It's hard to try one treatment and combine it with others at the same time, particularly if an experimental treatment is involved. As Carmen says, "Once you go down one treatment road, you're stuck. You can't go back."

Taking more than one experimental drug is, at best, questionable, and at worst, life-threatening. The person we love may choose AZT, for example. But this may rule out taking an experimental drug that may really help—one, in fact, that may become the cure for AIDS. In this situation, even extensive medical knowledge may not help. Instead, it may lead to an information overload. Absorbing all this information and coming up with rational answers that *feel* right are major tasks caregivers face in Stage Two.

Codependence

When our life is based solely on the well-being of the people we care for, we can remember that this is codependence. And the most subtle cues can trigger codependent responses.

This is part of Mark's experience with Dan: "He coughs during the night; I wonder if he has pneumonia. He's tired; I wonder if he has cancer." Underlying it is the persistent question, "What will I do without him?"

Mark answers this question by learning to adapt. Remembering that he's powerless over AIDS, he comes to hear those coughs without taking responsibility for them. His response is simply, "I'll do the best I can. I'll be here if Dan needs me. Staying up all night with him does neither of us any good." And with that, Mark goes back to sleep.

The same situation, however, prompts some caregivers to withdraw. Millie suppresses her feelings and becomes silent around Charlie. To herself she silently admits, *I can't take this anymore. I've done enough. I've had it with the resentments and blame.* She's preparing to be alone: *I have to be ready for when he goes. I feel like he's gone already.*

And even Charlie, in a way he may never consciously admit, is acting on the same idea: *I have to prepare her for when I'm gone. I'm going to withdraw now so she gets used to being alone.* In his own way, Charlie is taking charge of another person's well-being at the expense of his own. By doing so, he too is acting out the codependent script. A kind of unspoken suicide pact arises here: "If you die, I'll die." And even if that script isn't played out on a physical level, it can be acted out at an emotional level.

Codependence shows itself in other ways during Stage Two. One is flying between extremes. One moment comes the sacred pledge, "I'm going to be with you forever." Within hours, it's followed by, "I can't stand this house or you anymore. I'll just leave today." Overeating, drinking, drug use, refusing to take time alone—these, too, are extremes that deaden the pain of caregiving. They're also hallmarks of codependence.

Seeking Outside Support

This strategy is important because it signals a new orientation. For many caregivers, adapting marks the first time they look for formal helpers outside their network of family and friends. That help may come from a variety of sources: individual counseling, AIDS organizations, members of the clergy, professionally led support groups, or self-help groups. Among the last-mentioned are the array of Twelve Step programs, such as Alcoholics Anonymous, Narcotics Anonymous, Emotions Anonymous, Al-Anon, Alateen, Adult Children of Alcoholics, and Codependents Anonymous.

For many caregivers, seeking outside help means that a new stage in the caregiving journey is about to begin. With the support of others, some clarity and perspective starts to surface—even in the heart of pain.

Time truly does heal wounds. We recall Mark's description of Stage Two as plunging into cold water. After the initial shock, the body adjusts. This happens partly through automatic reactions, shivering, shuddering, and through conscious action, flailing arms, kicking legs. With such responses, the sensation of discomfort decreases. Through scores of subtle, internal changes, the body temperature returns to normal. The process takes time, and it's subtle. Even so, the body adapts.

Something like this happens in Stage Two. Over time, we come to grips with the discovery of AIDS. Sometimes this requires major, life-wrenching change. Just as often, though, adapting calls for gradual and subtle adjustments in the daily routine. Together, both kinds of change somehow make things regular. Even though life is changed forever, we can reasonably speak of a new routine. We've moved into a new stage; we've begun to coast.

CHAPTER 5

Stage Three: Coasting — Living with AIDS

Millie was a ten, not a Bo Derek "10," but a number ten bowling pin—an inconspicuous pin at first, but often left standing after all the others had been knocked down. Over the twenty-seven years of marriage to Charlie, twenty-five years of his alcoholism, and fifteen years of Al-Anon, she had learned coping and survival skills. These, coupled with what she was learning at AIDS Caregivers' support groups, made life with Charlie bearable. But that was it—just bearable.

Charlie had become cold and phlegmatic, like seaweed. Their relationship seemed shipwrecked on the shoals of his indifference, and a part of Charlie's coping mechanism was getting drunk. That made things even worse. He drank mostly on weekends—time he had once spent with his daughter and granddaughter. When his new grandson was born, it was Millie who spent most of the day with mother and baby. Charlie opted to go out, buy a bottle, come home, drink, and cry. He refused the invitation to come see his new grandson. He would not settle for seeing the boy only through protective glass shields in the maternity ward.

While Millie visited the hospital, she used the opportunity to lecture Charlene and Odell about AIDS and the special need Charlie now had for love and acceptance. Odell sym-

pathized, but would not budge from his position. "You know how kids pick things up," drawled Odell. "They just can't visit Charlie."

Charlie refused to see Charlene as long as she deprived him of his grandchildren. And that was fine with Odell. Charlie felt betrayed and resentful toward Millie for going over to Charlene's house, even though Millie explained that one of the purposes of her visits was to "soften up" their daughter. Charlie would leave the house when Charlene came to visit Millie; he'd go off to a saloon, using the whole situation as an excuse to drink. Soon Millie began to discourage Charlene's visits. She knew the effects they had on Charlie. Depriving herself of Charlene's company was her way of controlling Charlie's drinking.

Millie kept on attending AIDS Caregivers' support groups and Al-Anon, while Charlie steadfastly boycotted all meetings. He'd stopped going to his AA group long ago. He was getting sicker—thinner, weaker, and more insular. And Millie was simply surviving.

* * * * *

When Dan was first diagnosed with AIDS, he refused to buy green bananas at the supermarket. "Maybe I don't have that much time," he'd say. On trips back home to Boston, he'd make the obligatory stop at Filene's Basement. At first, he'd only buy slippers, pajamas, robes—things he'd need in hospitals or sickrooms. He'd pass up the designer suits drastically reduced in price. "I won't be needing suits," he'd say to Mark. Mark would get annoyed and lecture Dan about the power of positive thinking and Louise Hay's books on self-healing.

After fourteen months of survival, Mark had finally convinced Dan that there was life after AIDS. The angel of death was not necessarily at Dan's doorstep. It took Dan those fourteen months to trust that this was true. With that change in attitude, Dan and Mark could start coasting.

Dan looked upon death as a dark and indiscernible longitude encircling the secret geography of the earth. The subject of his own death brought two responses: it filled him with pleasant reveries of journeys both imminent and surprising, or it filled him with sorrow at the thought of leaving his beloved Mark behind.

Discussion with Mark about the first response was always vague, out of necessity. After all, who knew what to expect? Discussion about the second response was usually avoided, because it brought tears. "Why make ourselves miserable thinking about endings?" Dan would say. "Don't say 'dead'; say 'sleeping.' " Mark, on the other hand, wanted to confront those feelings of loss. So he'd depend on the ears and good counsel of Ellen, Sherman, and his AA sponsor. This compromise, reached with a therapist's help, worked for them.

Both men became more spiritual. Mark attended AA regularly and counted on his Higher Power for strength. Dan attended church regularly and openly professed a belief in God. But still, he embraced more exotic prescriptives of the Spirit, more vivid tonics to add character to his view of the world. He consulted channelers, mediums, and herbalists, and interrogated the Ouija board.

Their lives were full now. They included new routines: blood tests and party invitations; visits to the doctor and trips to Europe (India was off limits because of Dan's compromised immune system); treatments by day and concerts by night. Life together was a paradox of contrasts. They made the most of it, living in the moment—at least in the week.

* * * * *

If the phone was not ringing off the hook, Carmen's doorbell was buzzing. NA friends or AIDS activists would call or come to the tiny apartment to plan AIDS presentations with Carmen. Carmen loved the positive reinforcement and "stardom." She'd always wanted to be the center of attention. AIDS had given her the opportunity to "shine," to warn, to speak to groups, to teach. She'd learned through NA and PLWA (Persons Living with AIDS) support groups that she could have a lot of influence on her own life. For too long she lacked the nerve to star in her own show. Now she wanted to be both star and director. Oddly enough, since AIDS entered her life, she felt more complete than ever before.

Through all this Yolanda, unpleasingly plump, twenty-nine and unnoticed, would look on with disapproval. She'd try to limit Carmen's public presentations. "You have a family to raise Carmen," she'd say "They should come first." Or, "Spend more time with Inez and little Xavier. They need you more than the AIDS groups."

"I spend plenty of time with my kids," Carmen shot back defensively. "I need to get out more."

Inez had assumed all the household responsibilities and most of the care for her brother after school. She was used to listening to Yolanda and Carmen arguing. She was glad that her mother was clean, sober, and staying away from Xavier and his friends. But she couldn't help feeling resentful. Carmen's new life was causing her to once again be away from the family. Inez hungered for her mother's love and was almost relieved when Carmen was too ill to go out. The time Carmen spent at home, submerged in self-pity and blankets, at least allowed Inez to have her mother to herself. "I love you, Mama," Inez said over and over again as she combed her mother's hair.

Inez and Yolanda both found they got vicarious thrills out of Carmen's "stardom." They enjoyed being introduced to audiences, especially when Carmen was on a big stage or in a large auditorium. And after the meetings, they enjoyed the swarms of people wishing them well. Hermenia stayed at *home. It had taken Carmen months to convince her mother that it was okay for her to be doing what she was doing—being a crusader against needle sharing and AIDS. At least that battle was over. But at home, discussion about Carmen's illness was prohibited.*

Between food stamps, Medicaid, contributions, and small stipends for Carmen's speaking engagements, the family was surviving—barely, but still getting by.

* * * * *

COASTING AS A PARADOX

Coasting signals a new stage in life with AIDS. If adapting is taking steps to "normalize the insanity," then coasting is living with the results of those steps. In coasting, the road is straighter, smoother, with fewer bumps and curves. As Mark says, "What was a shock and a tragedy at first is now a regular part of our lives. We do everything we used to do—well, almost everything. It's just that our old activities have some new twists."

Coasting in Stage Three is different than adapting in Stage Two. We can see that difference by comparing the tasks in each stage.

Achieving Balance Between Two Sets of Demands

In Stage Two, people experience major change. Their emotions pass through a range of extremes. Their life circumstances change totally. Adapting is about making those changes. With it there's often subtle denial, an irrational hope that the diagnosis of AIDS was some kind of freak mistake.

As we struggle to adapt in Stage Two, emotions of sadness, pity, and fear may dominate our life. That may leave us with little energy for work, friends, or household tasks.

Our goal in Stage Two was to work with two sets of

demands: the demands from the outside world, and the demands from inside us—our emotions. The healing response is to balance these two sets of demands. Focusing only on the demands of the world can degenerate into denial. But focusing only on the maelstrom of our emotions can mean codependence. It's like tuning a guitar string: We tighten it a little, then loosen it. By experimenting, we find the proper tension between our private and public self, our inside life and outside life. That's the business of Stage Two.

In Stage Three, we caregivers and our loved ones have been living with major changes for a while. There's no doubt that AIDS is part of everyday reality. And for now, at least, the major decisions have been made: who to tell about the diagnosis, where to live, which doctor to see, how much to work, what treatments to take, how to go on. In Stage Two, we work to achieve a fragile and tentative balance. In Stage Three that balance is more or less in place, and we're just fine-tuning it. We pick up and go about the business of living.

Healing Responses

Stage Three also brings a certain matter-of-factness about living with AIDS. This pushes us to a new level of relationship with the people we care for. Our emotions are more subdued; we've gained some perspective. We may not talk about AIDS all that much. Some caregivers and their loved ones even develop a kind of short-hand language, a code for talking about AIDS, especially in public. One casual phrase, glance, or facial expression may say all we need to say for the moment. Dan and Mark refer to it as the "AGE." Carmen's family members just roll their eyes and mouth the word "AIDS" without making a sound.

In one way, this stage feels like a partial numbness to AIDS. This is not denying or avoiding the fact. Rather, coasting means just moving through that fact as part of the daily routine, much as we'd drive at night through a light fog. We can even talk about relaxing in the face of AIDS, of truly living with AIDS.

The caregivers in our vignettes give examples of this behavior. When Carmen whines, "I don't want to take my medicine," Yolanda's response is level — no shock or anger — just, "I know, but you must go ahead and take it."

Dan and Mark plan for weeks to attend a friend's birthday party. But on that night, Dan's feeling sick with exhaustion, diarrhea. So they spend the evening at home, reading by the fire.

And Millie admits the fact that Charlie doesn't talk anymore. "Sure, it was nice when he did talk," she says, "but life goes on." She simply repeats this adage to her counselor without comment or visible feeling.

In each case, the events that aroused our deepest fears in Stages One and Two no longer have the same power. Yes, the pain and fear are there, yet they seem familiar. We're used to it. We know it inside and out. We wish it were different, but we know that wishing changes nothing.

This kind of response can be healing. As caregivers, we have to go to work every day. We have to pay the bills. We have to go out in public. We have to get on with things; we can't cry all the time. We need to get on with our life.

"I have a slight touch of AIDS" is a phrase that captures the lighthearted part of Stage Three. And it can represent a healthy response. There's an easiness, a humor about it. There's casual acknowledgement of AIDS, even acceptance. After all, it's only a "slight touch." Yes, we know there's really no such thing as a slight touch of AIDS. Still, this way of referring to AIDS admits the fact without letting it overpower us. AIDS is a serious matter but no longer a cosmic event. It simply *is*.

Through all of this, the chronic sadness is still there. So is a low level of grief. Even the word *AIDS* casually mentioned in a television newscast evokes a visceral response. Indeed, it's still healthy—even necessary—to feel that chronic sadness or grief sometimes.

Coasting Over the "Blips"

With Stage Three, however, comes more perspective, some loosening of anxiety. Sadness, bitterness, pain—all those are present like a dark cloud. But life is regular: We eat; we sleep; we go to work. Perhaps we travel and do some of the things we dreamed about. And even though there's this sort of chronic awfulness in the picture, we go on living.

Part of even healthy coasting, though, is experiencing some static, some "blips" along the way. Sometimes it's not a comfortable coast. When we look closely, we'll see some bumps on that straight line on the graph. And for good reason. After all, on one level the reality is devastating.

So as caregivers, we live each conscious moment with a chronic level of distress. And at the same time, things are stable, regular, and even routine. When people ask how we're doing, "I'm doing rotten" and "I'm doing fine" are both honest and appropriate answers. There's really no such thing as coasting, but there is. Both statements are true, and this paradox is the heart of Stage Three.

WHAT HAPPENS IN COASTING

As we saw in Stage Two, adapting involves certain strategies and events. These will be as varied as the people involved. We can say the same things about coasting in Stage Three. Again, we will list common events here without labeling them as positive or negative.

Getting Used to a Changed Lifestyle

The lifestyle changes that began in Stage Two may continue well into the coasting stage. Among them may be more travel or vacations, new homes or apartments, different jobs, new job tasks, or reduced hours at work. By the time we reach Stage Three, however, most of those changes are in place. We may even have enough perspective to evaluate them. In doing so, we may decide on more far-reaching changes for the future. Or, we might choose to back off for now and just settle into a routine.

Every change raises relationship issues. For example, Millie returns to work to bolster the family budget, and she resents it. "Living with Charlie's moods, his silence, isn't that enough? Do I have to work too?" Charlie knows what Millie's thinking, though he doesn't say anything in response. Yet his silence is a response. Through silence, Charlie says something about his relationship with Millie: AIDS is off limits for discussion. We've been married for years, but that doesn't mean we have to talk about everything. If you feel angry about returning to work, that's tough. For Charlie and Millie, life goes on despite the deafening silence, and that's their style of coasting.

Dan and Mark have a different style. Dan has cut back to part time at his job, while Mark works more. Dan admits this is an economic necessity, but he struggles with it. For now Dan depends on Mark not only financially but emotionally as well.

Part of coasting for Dan and Mark is talking about this relationship issue: They negotiate and fine-tune their decisions about working. The discussions can be heated, and sometimes lots of feelings surface. Mark decides to work more hours. Yet Dan, who has cut back to part time at his job, wants more of Mark's time. "After all," says Dan, "I may not live much longer." At first those words pierce Mark like a dagger. After talking about it, though, they reach agreement. "I'll try and work less," says Mark, "if you'll try to understand when I have to work more."

"Our conversations about work are like an occasional pothole on a smoothly paved highway," says Mark. "Once in awhile the car hits those bumps, and it jars us a little. Yet we keep driving on." That ability to "keep driving on" is the hall-mark of coasting.

Inez is coasting too. She tires of all the cooking, cleaning, and "grown-up" work she has to do while Carmen goes to Narcotics Anonymous meetings and support groups. It reminds Inez of the times her mother was using drugs. Then, Carmen was often gone from the house. And even when her mother was at home, she was cold, distant, and unavailable. Even so, Inez reminds herself that Carmen is gone for a different reason now. "When she's home, I love spending time with her," says Inez. "Sometimes I get to hear her speeches, and that's fun. And the best thing is that Mama is clean. She's off drugs, and she's alive."

Experiencing Limits

Here the focus is on what we cannot do. "We don't stay out late anymore," says Mark. "We dared to stay up until midnight last night. Dan will pay for it in the morning! And so will I. When he feels bad, I feel bad."

Millie notes that the family income will suffer as Charlie takes more time off work. And the limits this imposes are written right into her menu; it means tuna casserole instead of steak suppers. It means closing the charge accounts. It means taking two hours to darn socks or reverse the collars on Charlie's shirts instead of replacing them. "But after all," says Millie, "we don't need many new clothes. He's in pajamas so much of the time anyway."

Again, Millie reports the facts with little feeling. For now, she's adjusted to the limits—or rather, resigned to them.

For Carmen, living with limits is hard. In one sense, her life is better than ever before. She's sober and she relishes her reputation as an energetic and colorful speaker. Yet Carmen is sick with AIDS. She needs her medication. And both those facts are hard for her to stomach. Instead of admitting these limits openly, Carmen depends on her caregivers. It's Yolanda's and Inez's job to make sure Carmen drinks enough water, gets enough rest, and takes her AZT on schedule. Yet none of them talk about this openly; it's all done with a glance, a nudge, or a whisper.

Feeling Mixed-Up Emotions

In both Stages One and Two, our emotions are affected. This is just as true in Stage Three. As mentioned earlier, the hallmark of Stage Three is a paradox — "I feel rotten" and "I feel fine." This shows up in emotions that contradict each other. Anger, sadness, and shame alternate moment-by-moment with lightness, detachment, joy, or humor.

Positive and negative emotions coexist, almost in the same instant. Yolanda screams at Carmen for talking about using drugs again. But that anger mixes with tenderness and humor: "I'm really angry at you because I don't want you to be sick. And besides, you turkey, if you're sick *I* have to stay up with you at the hospital and take care of your brats at home." The tenderness in Yolanda's eyes belies her words.

Mark's heart sinks when he thinks for a moment about Dan's sore legs. That symptom is a sign of something, though none of the doctors are sure. Dan counters that concern with humor. "If it's a brain tumor, we'll know soon enough," he quips. "Just don't forget to buy me a bigger hat." They laugh, exchange a loving glance, and the moment passes — no tears, no profound changes.

Changing Relationships with Friends

Relationships with friends evolve in ways we can't predict when they learn that our loved one has AIDS. This is true whether or not AIDS is openly discussed with friends.

Some friends know about the diagnosis but don't want to talk about it — so they don't. Even broaching the subject makes them feel uncomfortable. For people with AIDS and their caregivers, this often becomes a second level of secrecy: "I know they know. They know I know they know, but we don't talk about it much."

Silence about AIDS has a variety of meanings. With some friends there's a stinging denial that underlies even the most intimate conversation about other matters. That kind of silence can hurt.

With other friends there's a more natural silence that makes sense.

"How is Dan?"

"Fine except for a slight touch of AIDS."

That's a meaningful exchange between Mark and his buddy, Sherman. There's no need to detail the pain, frustration, or the latest bout of diarrhea. None of those things are new. Dan's alive and relatively well – that's what counts. And that's what Sherman wants to know. "After all," notes Mark, "what can Sherman say, really? It's the same reason Dan and I don't talk about AIDS all the time. We both admit it's part of our lives, but what more can we say?"

What happens to relationships with people who don't know about AIDS – parents, for example? They'll ask, "How are you? . . . Why are you moving? . . . Why are you cutting back at work?" Because we care for someone with a socially unacceptable disease, we might feel like retreating to half-truths. We talk about needing a change, wanting to get more out of life, but we don't tell them about AIDS, the real reason. That raises several questions: "What toll does days, months, or years of telling limited truths take on a relationship? And what does it do to us?" These are questions for us to keep asking, even when we have few answers.

Another issue is keeping all the stories straight. It becomes complicated to sort out who knows and who doesn't. When Mark sees family and friends, the same web of questions always comes up: "Who am I going to see at that party tonight? . . . Who suspects, and who really knows about

Dan's AIDS? . . . What can I say to Phyllis, Dan's mom? . . . What if she knows more than I think she knows? . . . Has she talked about this when we're not around?" Mark yearns to be open and honest. At the same time, he knows better than to go against Dan's wish for privacy and risk upsetting him.

Searching for Someone Who Will Listen

What can we do when pain and sadness come up for us but not for the people we care for? Our emotions have their own timetable, and our negative feelings may arise at the "wrong" times for the person with AIDS. For example, Mark says:

> *I feel rotten tonight. But is it right to dump this on Dan? I want to talk to someone, but I'll just ruin his evening if I talk about it. He's got enough of a load already.*
>
> *Does this mean I can never really be honest with him again? Who else can I talk to? And what will I say? It's a real problem. If I call my sponsor for support, Dan may feel slighted and hurt. But if I do talk to him, he'll feel overloaded. I feel like I love him more than he loves me. I'm the caregiver, but who cares for me?*

For Millie, the issues are similar:

> *When Charlie doesn't take care of himself—he never really does—I can't stand it. When he doesn't take his medicine, I get upset. When he doesn't rest, I feel tired and can't even get the housework done. And who's there when I want to talk? Who can I turn to? That's the question nobody ever answers for me.*

Sometimes the "solution" is to simply beat back the sadness, anger, or fear; we suppress our feelings. This is Millie's course: "Better that I say nothing. After all, Charlie is the one who's really sick."

For many of us, another choice is finding a neutral, committed helper—someone who's neither family nor a personal friend. Counseling, both joint and individual, can help many caregivers during Stage Three. Doctors, therapists, members of the clergy, self-help groups, AIDS support groups—all may be sources of help. And as caregivers, our use of these services may deepen during coasting.

Support groups, such as those based on the Twelve Steps of Alcoholics Anonymous, may help us feel calmer, more grounded. Even so, any group raises a frightening issue for caregivers like Millie: "Who in the group should know that Charlie has AIDS? . . . Will anyone I tell really keep it to themselves? Or will the word spread, and will the secret end up in my face?"

Often we have no clear answers. Many caregivers decide to avoid any risk with a blanket decision—they tell no one. The reaction to this decision varies. Some caregivers feel relieved, knowing that the diagnosis is a safely kept secret. And yet others sense a real loss. They feel that even their efforts to heal themselves are restrained by silence.

Undergoing Treatment

In Stage Three we've made the major decisions about getting treatment for AIDS. At this point, the people in our vignettes are "taking their medicine." Carmen and Charlie are on AZT. This means frequent blood tests, which Charlie describes as "weekly assaults on my veins by those blood letters, the nurses." Dan is taking an experimental drug Mark found for him through a friend, a doctor in Key West. This requires injections every other day, first thing in the morning. That day always starts the same way, with shouts of protest from Dan. Mark threatens to "use a rusty needle" if Dan doesn't settle down. And finally Dan submits, with resignation and grudging acceptance.

During Stage Three, the need for treatment, the side-effects, and the medical follow-up become regular too.

Caregivers coast along in their role as "pill-pusher" or "shot-giver." Our role is that of watchdog. Like Millie, Yolanda, and even Inez, we remind or scold: "Did you take your 4:00 P.M. dose?" Charlie and Carmen, sharing some of the same rebellious nature, often snap back: "Of course. Don't you trust me?"

Along with this comes a list of related tasks: Finding some source to pay for the most costly treatments, filling prescriptions, calling the doctor, or asking for a smaller dose of medication or added drugs to counteract the side-effects everyone grows to expect, such as nausea, diarrhea, sleepiness, irritability. Yet, it's all in a day's work. We expect it. The whole routine is predictable, even in its unpredictability.

As noted in Stage Two, we face a bewildering array of traditional and non-traditional treatments for AIDS. Caregivers and people with AIDS differ widely in their response to this fact. One extreme is to try everything possible. The other extreme is to be passive, to take whatever the doctor gives and pray for freedom from side-effects. In between these extremes, many people with AIDS and their caregivers find a bargain with uncertainty.

During Stage Three, some caregivers and people with AIDS may even abandon the whole path of traditional Western medicine. Instead, they turn to religion or spirituality for help. For some, this means traditional Western religious creeds. For others, it means pushing to the far edges of metaphysics. Approaches that seemed unscientific, occult, or esoteric before life with AIDS now find a hearing. Examples could be listed by the hundreds: attitudinal healing, visualization, various brands of meditation, yoga, "channeled" texts such as the *Course in Miracles*, those from Louise Hay, and more (see Appendix Four, Recommended Materials on AIDS and Caregiving, page 226–227). All are attempts to modulate the mind and emotions, thereby healing the body.

Some of us will find help in such sources—strength that will help us through the stages of discovery, adapting, and coping. Yet no treatment, traditional or experimental, has guarantees. We can say only one sure thing about life with AIDS: It's uncertain. It's unpredictable. It means life can totally change at any minute. And this fact may move us into collisions and Stage Four—whether we're prepared for it or not.

CHAPTER 6

Stage Four: Colliding— Facing Crisis

Millie was reflecting on the past two months of her life. Clearly, they were the worst months she'd ever experienced. Charlie confessed, while in the hospital, that he'd had sexual relationships with prostitutes while he was on business trips. Millie confessed that she had broken her vow of secrecy about Charlie's disease. And she began to recognize that a film of distrust, like wispy spores on aging marmalade, had clouded their marriage.

The past two months—the intensive care unit vigil, the uncertainty—had been living hell. She was pleased that Charlene had reconciled with her father and that he had been able to meet and hold his grandson, who was almost one year old before Charlie entered the hospital for the last time.

Odell, looking awkward and uncomfortable in a suit and tie, exited the limousine first, followed by Millie and Charlene. The cemetery was an Indian summer showpiece, a gallery of bronzes, goldenrods, and jades. Millie was burying her husband. Thoughts ran through her mind as she walked to the newly purchased family plot. Was Charlie's AIDS a result of the blood transfusion or was his death the result of infidelity? She hated that she would never know.

What was she going to do without Charlie? Could she ever forgive him for his infidelity? What was widowhood going to be like? How could she support herself? Would she have to give up the house? She was a financial illiterate and she knew it. How would her friends respond to her now that they knew Charlie had died of AIDS? Could she ever forgive her son-in-law for the heartaches he'd caused the family during Charlie's illness? The grave loomed in front of her and she thought she would faint.

* * * * *

Dan was on the phone to his friend, Rowland, in New York complaining about the nurses. Dan had been in the hospital for six days with high fevers and night sweats. He'd even become delirious for a time. Today, though, he was feeling a little better.

"There is a night nurse named Ms. Tarbox, and she certainly can't be described as Franciscan in her sensitivity and tenderness toward her fellow human beings. She overheard me cursing her under my breath and now she's retaliating when she sticks me with the needles. Finally, I'm a member of the IV League, Rowland; it's feeding me constantly. I was dehydrated. There is another nurse, Mrs. Rose Flower, who's so old she defies the actuarial tables. If I want to ensure twenty minutes of privacy I signal for the nurse."

Dan and Rowland's phone conversation was cut short when Mark walked in. His face said "urgent." Mark told Dan that Dan had been very sick, with temperatures of 104 for five days. At one point, Dan had been delirious. Phyllis, Dan's mother, had called earlier that day to talk to her son. Mark had felt that he had no choice but to tell her that Dan was in the hospital. And now Phyllis was outside the room waiting to come in.

Dan turned pale and weak. The two years of secrecy were over—or were they? What fabrication could he weave to prevent his mother from finding out the truth? "What does she know?" squeaked Dan, barely able to speak.

"*Everything,*" *said Mark.* "*I told her everything: AIDS, gay, us—everything. Dan, she was surprisingly rational and insisted on coming right out. She called early this morning and now she's here.*"

Dan shuddered. "*How could you do that when you promised not to?*" *shouted Dan.* "*I'll never forgive you!*"

Just then Phyllis burst in. She was a very put-together woman, the sort you'd guess to be around forty-five, then later decide is sixty and diligent. She was a far cry from other women of her generation. She was svelte though not cadaverous and used makeup to flattering effect. "*Hello son,*" *she said with concern.* "*How are you?*"

"*I'm okay, Mom. I just have a slight touch of AIDS.*"

Phyllis did not see the humor. "*Don't make light of this. Where is your doctor and when can I see him?*" *she asked imperiously.* "*Is he any good?*"

Mark noticed that Phyllis's hair looked more persimmon-colored than usual. But he had not commented as mother and son talked, at first coolly, then heatedly. She made her conservative views clear. Mark quietly slipped out and instructed Nurse Tarbox to end the fracas. "*I'm sorry, Mrs. DeLyon. Dan has to rest now,*" *she said.* "*You'll be able to visit him tomorrow.*"

"*I flew all the way from Boston to be with my son, and no one is going to tell me to leave,*" *Phyllis said to the nurse.* "*Get out of here and leave us alone.*"

Dan and Mark just looked at each other as the nurse bolted to get her supervisor. With that one look, Mark's insides told him he was in for a rough stint. How was he going to handle this steamroller who was his mother-in-law? How was he going to live with her during Dan's convalescence and recuperation? How would Dan handle Mark's spilling the beans?

* * * * *

Over Hermenia's, Inez's, and particularly Yolanda's vehement objections, Carmen called Xavier to tell him that little Xavier had been taken to the hospital. The boy had a fever and had been coughing nonstop for two days. She was calling not because she expected help of any kind from Xavier, but because he was the boy's father, after all. Xavier, who was usually distant, seemed to register genuine concern and emotion over the bad news. He made arrangements to come by the apartment to pick her up and to go to the hospital.

Yolanda and Inez went through a litany of warnings about Xavier's bad influence. Yolanda knew that Carmen and Xavier were still attracted to each other. She feared that this meeting, and the time Carmen and Xavier spent in the hospital together, would undo months of Carmen's sobriety and clean time.

But despite their concerns about Carmen, Inez and Yolanda fretted for the baby. "He's so tiny," said Inez. "Is he going to die?" she asked through a flood of tears.

"Shut up!" Yolanda shrieked. "Don't you say such a thing, you little fool!"

Yolanda regretted the words as soon as they erupted. "I'm sorry, baby. I didn't mean it. We're all upset."

The three women sat together as the buzzer rang. Xavier had sense enough to wait for Carmen downstairs on the stoop.

While Carmen and Xavier went to the hospital, Inez and Yolanda commiserated about the future, speculating about the new developments: the baby's illness, and Xavier's arrival back on the scene. Everything had been going so well. Carmen had been clean, sober. Inez had settled into an acceptable routine of domestic drudgery, child care, and school work. Hermenia had picked up a cleaning job Wednesday evenings and weekends to help make ends meet. Yes, everything had been going well—until now.

There was more. Hermenia later told Carmen, Inez, and

Yolanda that the tenants in the building had signed a petition to evict Carmen, Inez, and little Xavier. The tenants had put up with measles and hepatitis epidemics in the building. But now, in the face of little Xavier's illness, they'd had enough. The tenants feared contagion. They were ready and able to make life even more miserable for Carmen and her family if she didn't move.

Within days Carmen and Inez were living with Yolanda, which placed an even bigger burden on Yolanda. But she knew choices were non-existent for Carmen and Inez. So Yolanda resigned herself to sharing the two small rooms she had called her own. "After all, what else can I do?" Yolanda asked as she went through her closet and drawers, trying to make room for her new roommates.

Carmen thought the living conditions were bad at her mother's place; they were even worse at Yolanda's cracker-box apartment. Carmen, sick at heart over her son's worsening pneumonia, spent many nights away from the apartment, at Xavier's. She needed release from the claustrophobia she felt at Yolanda's. And when her mom was out, Inez hardly slept. Instead, she worried the night away.

* * * * *

COLLISIONS: BACK TO SQUARE ONE

Stage Four reaffirms a central fact: the "balance" achieved in Stage Three can be precarious at best. Unexpected events—collisions—might rob us of whatever serenity we've achieved. We may even feel like we're beaten back into many Stage One emotions: sadness, fear, shock, shame, and all the rest. Things are coming apart again, just when they seemed to be going all right.

What are collisions? Some examples help define the term:

- Someone new finds out our loved one has AIDS. Confidentiality is breached.
- Our loved one develops pneumonia, cancer, or another life-threatening condition.
- We, the caregiver, test positive for HIV.
- We lose our apartment, our job, or our insurance because the person we live with has AIDS.
- We're ostracized at work. Friends stop calling. Relatives cut off contact. Neighbors reject us.
- We have to declare bankruptcy because of high medical bills.
- We divorce, leave, or separate from the person with AIDS.
- A friend or member of our support group dies from AIDS.
- Our loved one dies.

Clearly, the people in our vignettes experience collisions. Charlie dies, and before he does, he admits his infidelity. Millie must not only mourn Charlie but take in these revelations as well. Anger, shock, grief, despair, panic—all these emotions are alive inside her.

Dan enters the hospital, and even there he faces stigma. Beyond this, he's forced into a confrontation with his mother—an event he's steadfastly avoided for two years.

Stigma is also a factor for Carmen's family. In the face of their neighbors' rage and rejection, they flee to Yolanda's tiny apartment. Carmen spends more time with Xavier, which threatens Carmen's hard-won sobriety and widens the emotional gap between she and her family. On top of it all, little Xavier now has AIDS and may die.

Explosions on the "Highway"

Collisions are crises. These events threaten the painstaking work of earlier stages: discovery, adapting, and coasting. Our analogy for caregiving is that of a journey, a path, or a trip. If that's true, then collisions are far more than detours or potholes on the road. Instead, they're places where explosions have destroyed the highway. They're like crashing into a brick wall. They're like getting lost and finding out you're in a spot that's not on your map. With collisions you may feel forced to turn around, retrace your steps—even start the trip over again.

With collisions we're faced with redefining relationships, especially with the people we care for. Old issues resurface; buried pain comes to life again. What do we really feel for each other? Do we divorce? Do we separate? Do we just maintain? Do we take any action at all? What can we really do about this, anyway? Can we ever make it through this?

Uncertainty is a constant, underlying concern in Stage Four. The people we care for could die tomorrow. They could live for a year, two years, five years. Or they could be with us for decades. Add to this the unique problems posed by AIDS: stigma, shame, discrimination. We confronted these in Stage One. In Stage Four we may face them again, and with renewed force.

Often collisions are external events: attending funerals, going to the hospital, discovering that treatment produces a major side-effect. The sheer drama of these events can be enough to immerse us in the old, aching pain. The tentative truce we struck with AIDS has been shattered. Our emotions are on the battlefield again.

The crucial point is not the external event but its emotional impact. For that reason, what may be a collision for one caregiver is only a slight detour for another. Everything depends on how we, as individuals, react.

At unexpected moments, such reactions can claim us with a savage force. All the techniques we've used to silence or soften their blow may suddenly fail. And once again we face a whole new round of discovery and adapting—stages we thought we'd completed.

Collisions aren't always "outside" events that shatter our external circumstances. For some caregivers, collisions are internal events. They're contractions of the heart, not always visible to others:

- Realizing that AIDS has cut off any chance of achieving goals; seeing that AIDS has nullified the plans we've made
- Aching with nostalgia over the past and longing for a return to the days when everything was "normal"
- Feeling that the chance for a meaningful sex life has been cut off forever

With Stage Four we're reminded that the caregiver's path doesn't always go in a straight line. In fact, our journey is more like a circle or spiral. People recovering from chemical dependency talk of "recycling." This word points to slow, faltering attempts at reaching sobriety. Sometimes those attempts are marred by periods of relapse, of acting on the cravings to drink or use other drugs. For people in Twelve Step programs, this can literally mean taking several steps backwards—if not returning to the bottom.

With collisions in Stage Four, caregivers may likewise hit bottom again. Just when we're feeling confident about any gains we've made, it feels like we're left with nothing. We've lost any serenity we've achieved. We're back to square one.

SURVIVING AND RESPONDING TO COLLISIONS

Earlier we said that the main thing about collisions is their emotional impact. It's not the event that throws us into a collision—it's our *response* to that event. This fact defines the nature of collisions. At the same time, it also raises the possibility of surviving collisions, and even preventing them.

The potential for healing is present in every collision. As painful as this stage can be, it also puts the core life issues in strong perspective.

- A collision may puncture denial and allow us to accept the full reality of AIDS.
- Instead of despairing, collisions may lead us to reconcile with long alienated family members and friends.
- Stage Four may also help us reconcile with the loved one who has AIDS.
- Suffering at this stage may deepen our spiritual lives, push us into new insights, and reveal what's truly important to us.

Inner strength, commitment to health, and other gifts may surface out of stark emotional pain. As caregivers, we meditate, we pray, we call friends, we vent feelings—we use any coping method that allows us to survive without harming others. And each of us has a unique style of coping. Our reactions have their own pattern, their own texture.

What determines how we respond to a collision? Is it possible to reduce the force of impact? Even if we re-experience the pain of earlier stages, can we lessen its intensity or its duration? Can we reduce life-wrenching suffering to mere discomfort? Can we, in effect, buy "insurance" for collisions?

Here we've raised questions well beyond the scope of this chapter. Answering them calls on us to say much more. More specifically, it means explaining tools for acceptance. This is our focus in the chapters that follow.

PART THREE

TOOLS FOR ACCEPTANCE

Prologue

The history of psychology has given us many models of the human being. In this book, we find it useful to talk about three aspects of our selves: thoughts, feelings, and actions. These are the core, the most basic units in our experience of the world. And as a result, they are the things we "work" on to free ourselves from suffering and realize serenity.

Someone we love has AIDS. What can we do? Who will help *us?* And is there anything, after all, that can really help? How can we help ourselves? Does it even make sense to speak of acceptance?

In the wake of the AIDS diagnosis, many of us grope for a response—especially if we're in the grip of all the negative Stage One emotions. We can feel lost. In the worst moments, it seems, all outside support has vanished. Job, family, relationship with family and friends—will any of them survive this blow? All our familiar props in the world seem shattered. Emotionally, we are without a home.

Desperate for comfort, we turn inward. And what do we find there? We may be so paralyzed by fear, sadness, grief, or anger that we feel only an aching void. We may feel despairing and powerless. We simply have no idea where to turn, who to call, or what to do.

One premise of this book is that simple truths are sometimes the most healing. And in moments when we feel clouded, anxious, or lost, we can remember the simple answer to the central question: "Someone I love has AIDS; what can I do to accept this fact?" Our answer has four parts, each pointing to a specific response. We call them *phases:*

Phase A: Learning
Phase B: Working with Feelings
Phase C: Taking Action
Phase D: Acceptance

In the following pages, we devote a chapter to each kind of response.

Before doing so, we can underline two important points. First, *caregivers often move through these solutions in roughly the order we've laid out.* For many, learning comes first. Before working with feelings, it makes sense to gather information. In Stage One, this can mean learning that a loved one has AIDS and what that really means. In later stages the learning continues. We learn about insurance, wills, opportunistic infections that can result from AIDS, the health care system, things that weaken or strengthen the immune system—all these and more. In each case, our activity centers on gathering facts and coming to terms with whatever information we find. These draw on the intellect—the part of us that thinks, reasons, compares, judges, and evaluates.

Caregivers, however, often find that what they learn arouses deep emotions. Soon after gaining knowledge we ask, "How will this affect me and the person I love?" It's here that we must pause to open to our feelings and learn about them. As we saw in Part Two of this book, each stage in our caregiving journey typically involves certain patterns of emotion. We can respond in two primary ways: (1) experiencing those feelings as they come up, and (2) meeting those feelings with a healing response.

Once we've taken the edge off our feelings of sadness, fear, shock, or anger, we can move to the next response: taking action. In taking action, we build upon the first two responses. That is, in order to act, it first helps to learn; we must know what actions are appropriate. Working with feelings allows us to move beyond them—at least for the moment. Otherwise, strong negative feelings may leave us with little energy to change our daily lives. Finally, by completing the first three phases, we can approach acceptance, serenity, and peace.

It's not always true that caregivers move through these phases in this order. Moreover, we are not abnormal in any way if our journey detours or centers more on one phase than another. Some caregivers focus primarily on learning; others are more comfortable working with feelings. And for some, taking action is the most healing response.

In addition, listing four phases does not mean they are separate. In fact, they are related in many ways, over a whole range of time and behavior. For example, learning about AIDS can help us get a better handle on our feelings. Taking action increases our learning and moves us closer to acceptance. We offer this list of phases in the same spirit as our list of stages. They are neither a scientific description nor a straitjacket. Rather, they give us a way to make sense out of our experience. They give us a language for talking about caregiving—both to ourselves and to others. Because it promotes awareness, using this list of stages and the phases within each stage can promote our well-being.

The second major point about phases is this: *They occur at each stage of caring for a person with AIDS.* That is, we can learn, work with feelings, take action, and move toward acceptance within each stage. In fact, we can integrate these phases with each stage. Doing so gives us a more complete picture:

Stage One: Discovering
　Phases:
　　A. Learning
　　B. Working with Feelings
　　C. Taking Action
　　D. Acceptance

Stage Two: Adapting
  Phases:
    A. Learning
    B. Working with Feelings
    C. Taking Action
    D. Acceptance
Stage Three: Coasting
  Phases:
    A. Learning
    B. Working with Feelings
    C. Taking Action
    D. Acceptance
Stage Four: Colliding
  Phases:
    A. Learning
    B. Working with Feelings
    C. Taking Action
    D. Acceptance

With this map of the caregiver's journey sketched out, we will fill in more details about each phase.

CHAPTER 7

Phase A—Learning

Pouring over a limp, butter-softened copy of Gourmet *and taking assiduous notes, Millie waited for the other members of the AIDS support group. She did not just read* Gourmet, *which she really had never seen before; she studied it exhaustively. Charlie had been a meat and potatoes man and considered her bearnaise sauce a French plot to ruin perfectly good steak. She made a mental note to get an annual subscription.*

Millie was a survivor, and months ago she recognized the value of therapy and support groups. She immediately joined a bereavement group. Even though she was the only woman in the group among five gay men, she quickly fit in and made friends. She learned about gayness and the problems that gay men face. She learned about widowhood. She saw a commonality between her own widowhood and the loss experienced by the gay men. They were widowers born of the same storm. In their losses there was bonding. Millie and the gay men moved easily through each other's minds, trading easily in one another's idiom.

Millie uneasily learned about the household finances, and that she had no credit in her name. Millie had a history of adding two and two and coming up with varied results, so the finances were really a problem for her. She depended on some of the men in her group, along with her sister-in-law, to help her sort things through and actually establish credit.

* * * * *

Phyllis was a difficult woman. She had a history of reporting better business bureaus to other better business bureaus! Mark and Dan recognized this long ago, and now Mark was prepared to help Phyllis learn about gayness and AIDS. In the car, en route from the hospital to home, he brought up some books he'd picked up for her. Books like Loving Someone Gay, Family Matter, The Male Couple, and On Being Gay. Mark also told Phyllis that he'd take her to a PFLAG meeting (Parents and Friends of Lesbians and Gays) next Tuesday evening, and he told her about some AIDS support group meetings. "I've already made arrangements for us to go," said Mark. "You have a lot to learn about your son, his gayness, and this disease, Phyllis. I'm willing to make your stay here as comfortable, but as informative, as possible."

Phyllis glared at him with a look that, while not warm, told him that her inquisitive mind would be receptive to the information. But it wasn't going to be a picnic.

* * * * *

Carmen learned that spending time with Xavier meant eventually spending time with his friends and doing drugs or being tempted. Life there was a moral mud slide. Clearly, if she wanted to be clean and sober, she had to give up Xavier and everything he represented.

Little Xavier had been in the hospital for three and a half weeks with no signs of improvement. Carmen had finally started listening to the doctors when they visited — once, sometimes twice each day. She'd taken to asking questions, particularly of one of the Hispanic nurses, someone she found she could trust.

When faced with conflicting information about AIDS or gaps in her knowledge, Carmen and Yolanda read. They'd *ask more questions. And they'd pump the people at their support groups for any facts they could provide.*

* * * * *

Learning about AIDS can reduce the mystery and fear that the disease evokes in some of us. True, knowing the facts about AIDS — how it's transmitted, what it can do to the body, what treatments are currently used — does not in itself cure anyone. Even so, increasing our knowledge helps us develop a sense of control over our life. Knowing in advance about the course of a disease can reduce our surprise if symptoms develop. Arming ourselves with information about AIDS may help us prepare for what is to come.

Reading about AIDS and listening to well-informed people can also remove us temporarily from the "scene of the battle" — our raging emotions. Gathering and assimilating facts puts us in a clearer, more detached state of mind. In those moments, we're lifted above the details of our own circumstances.

For as we examine the growing literature on AIDS, we're reminded of the fundamental fact that we're not alone. Behind the articles, speeches, workshops, and seminars on AIDS there are people like us — people with AIDS and those who care for them. There are people getting sick, crying with each other, caring for each other, and people *living well* with AIDS.

When we learn about AIDS, we're observing, gathering data, thinking, and gaining understanding. We're processing the information and coming to our own conclusions. We're also freeing ourselves from the stereotypes, misinformation, and falsehoods that circulate about AIDS. If we don't, these ideas can lead to needless anxiety and complicate our task as caregivers.

In many cases, caregivers point to one step they used early in coming to terms with their loved one's AIDS: learning. "I started reading everything about AIDS I could," says Mark about the long hours he spent pouring over medical journals, books, and newspaper articles. "I wanted to get the facts. I figured the more I knew, the better caregiver I could be. What we know about AIDS is changing all the time, so it pays to stay on top of the latest research."

For Millie, Mark, and Yolanda, this step came in Stage Two: adapting. As the shame, anger, shock, and sadness softened, they asked, "What is this thing called AIDS? What does it do to people? How can it affect the person I love? And how will it affect me?" It's natural and helpful to seek answers to these questions. Doing so can help us become competent, compassionate caregivers.

HOW LEARNING CAN HELP US AS CAREGIVERS

Learning about AIDS can be a step toward healing and wholeness for us. This is true for several reasons. For one, seeking out the facts helps us put an end to our role as victims. We're no longer passive, helplessly waiting for illness to take its course. And when the people we care for start learning about AIDS, they're no longer cast in the role of victim either. They too are responding and taking part in their own health, not merely reacting to the latest event.

In seeking information, we can also become more objective. When we gather information, we can step back from AIDS and view it with some perspective. These moments can bring clarity and calm: we're no longer in panic or shock; we're no longer drowning in negative emotions. Instead, we're acting like researchers: carefully piecing together what is known, discovering what we don't know, and working patiently toward knowing more. With these things in mind, we can take the knowledge we gain—no matter how limited—and apply it to our situation.

Learning about AIDS bears out the observation made by the seventeenth century English philosopher, Francis Bacon, that "knowledge is power." We can discover a healing power in knowledge. It's a well-known fact that people with a chronic illness long for a diagnosis, a name for their condition. Merely being able to name a condition and list its symptoms does something to reduce its mystery.

To name is to gain power. Naming means that we've reduced the mystery of the illness. With a name came a realization for Millie: "We've learned enough about AIDS to label and describe it. Here's what our doctor knows about it. Others besides us have struggled with pneumocystis, and we're not alone. There are predictable symptoms, and something can be done about most of them. There is hope."

Furthermore, knowing something about the course of AIDS and its possible complications can reduce the element of surprise. We can learn, for example, that the person with AIDS may have some problems with memory and processing facts. This prepares us for behavior we might not understand otherwise from the person with AIDS, such as forgetting to take medication, needing to be reminded of an appointment, or not understanding what we try to say.

Such knowledge diffuses our own anxiety and helps us stay on top of our feelings about such "strange" behaviors. It can also avoid needless squabbles and tension in our relationships with the people we care for. As Mark says, "When Dan asks me to repeat things I've said, I can remind myself that he's not trying to be irritating or dependent. He just doesn't understand. And when he leaves in the middle of a party and says he needs to go lay down, I know he's coping with a reduced energy level. He's not being difficult or melodramatic. He just needs to rest. Now that I know this, I'm less likely to be upset or angry at him."

COMING TO TERMS
WITH THE AMOUNT OF INFORMATION

We may run into some roadblocks when gathering information. And we can resolve these if we're prepared for them. To begin, there's *so much* information about AIDS. The literature on AIDS is expanding daily, and so are the theories about the disease and treatments. What's more, our understanding of AIDS and the language we use to express it are changing almost as quickly.

Unfortunately, much of the current information is inaccurate, inflammatory, or contradictory. And as we survey the sources of this information, one reason becomes clear: these sources operate with a variety of motives, with some leading to superficial or sensational treatment of AIDS. Newspapers aim for accuracy, but not at the cost of decreasing sales. Scientists search for a cure, but they also compete for grant dollars and seek to advance their careers. Pharmaceutical companies work to make the latest drug available, but also strive for higher profits. Government officials promote public safety, but also court public opinion and face election contests. At the center of this maelstrom of motives are the people with AIDS and us, their loved ones, longing simply for health, recovery, and survival.

Some caregivers feel anxiety and frustration over these facts. They feel guilty about not being able to get through all the information on AIDS. They feel sad or angry when they can't penetrate the medical jargon. They feel cheated when discovering that the experts disagree. And they feel overwhelmed by the sheer volume of it all.

Another potential problem is *selective perception*, that is, seeing only the facts that fit what we feel. When learning that Charlie was infected with HIV, for example, Millie immediately read it as a death sentence. She focused on the statistics about death from AIDS, ignoring the survival rate and the stories of people who've experienced remission. She saw HIV illness and AIDS as one and the same, forgetting that a person who tests positive for HIV may never develop AIDS.

Millie needed the facts about AIDS. She also needed to talk with someone with a perspective on the facts—a perspective that includes possibility of survival. We can all benefit from that perspective.

MAPPING OUT THE INFORMATION ON AIDS

This situation calls for two things. First, we need a way to gain perspective on information about AIDS. We need some way to reduce the volume of data to a size we can manage — to filter out the overload. We need guidelines for gaining a balance of information about AIDS. With that balance, we can avoid gathering facts in ways that only reinforce our fears. Second, we need to find sources of information that we can trust.

One solution is working from a basic outline of what we need to know. This can be much like a class syllabus or an outline for a course we took in school. If we think of the stages of our journey as caregivers, then this outline is a map highlighting roadside stops. On our map we can list the major topics in our knowledge about AIDS. Working with such an outline, we'll learn what information to look for. We'll know, too, where there are gaps in our knowledge. And, as we learn new facts, we can add those facts to our outline. Knowing that there's a "place" to assign each fact can help us feel more at home with this mass of information.

Since this is not a book about the medical aspects of AIDS, we won't present those kind of details here. Several fine works exist that do provide this kind of information. Instead of duplicating their content, we've listed them under Recommended Materials on AIDS and Caregiving in Appendix Four (page 226–227). You'll also find a summary of key AIDS facts in this appendix. Our aim in this chapter is to list the broad categories in our present knowledge of AIDS. With the following outline, you can organize your fact gathering and gain perspective. Please note that it includes the whole spectrum of disease that may result from Human Immunodeficiency Virus (HIV) — the virus that may lead to AIDS.

How HIV disease is transmitted:
- Unsafe sexual behaviors
- Blood exchange, including needle sharing and tranfusions
- Risks posed by using alcohol and other drugs
- Transmission from mother to fetus

How HIV diseases affect the body:
- Effects on the immune system (T-cells)
- How diseases may develop
- Effects on the brain

Illnesses associated with HIV:
- Pneumonia
- Cancer (Kaposi's sarcoma, lymphoma)
- Other infections (protozoal, viral, fungal, bacterial)
- How illnesses may progress

Testing for HIV illness:
- Pre-test counseling
- Types of tests
- Discrimination that may result from testing
- Seeking out anonymous versus confidential testing

Preventing HIV illness:
- Avoiding transmission from intravenous drugs
- How to practice safer sex
- How to recover from chemical dependency

Treating HIV illness:
- Treating opportunistic infections
- Preventing opportunistic infections
- Using antiviral agents
- Stimulating the immune system
- Using vaccines
- Non-traditional treatments
- Side-effects
- Limitations of treatment

Survival:
- Does it happen
- How to maximize the chance of living longer

This outline is only one of many ways to organize this knowledge. You may include different topics or rearrange the topics included here. As caregivers we can construct our own maps: Millie's or Mark's map will be different from Yolanda's or Inez's. That's appropriate. Remember that our purpose is not to arrive at the perfect summary of AIDS; our goal is to be informed caregivers. Any way of organizing the facts we need to know is fine, as long as it moves us toward one goal: the ability to care without being consumed, overwhelmed, or victimized.

Above all, we seek a balanced picture about AIDS. With that perspective, we can see our task not as watching someone suffer or die from AIDS. Instead, we'll know that our task as caregivers is helping someone *live* with AIDS.

COPING WITH MISINFORMATION

A big part of our job in the learning stage is to seek out information. Equally important, though, is weeding out the misinformation, inaccuracies, and half-truths currently circulating about AIDS. Because they distort our knowledge of AIDS, they can also have a negative effect on our feelings and actions as caregivers.

Since much of what we'll learn about AIDS comes from television and newspapers, it makes sense to take a critical look at these sources of information. Jody Powell, White House press secretary under former president Jimmy Carter, underscored this point. "Reporters aren't perfect," he points out. "They are usually facing tight deadlines, and don't always have the time and medical expertise to prepare themselves adequately to cover the issue."[1]

Powell, writing in *You Can Do Something About AIDS*,

reminds us to beware of certain "buzzwords" that affect reporting about AIDS:

- *Bodily fluids*—Too often the mention of this phrase leads people to think that *any* bodily fluid can transmit HIV. It's important to note that only semen, vaginal fluids, and blood have been shown to transmit the virus.
- *General population*—This phrase segregates people into two rigid classes: those who are HIV positive and the rest who are not. Powell responds this way: "Everyone who has AIDS—regardless of sexual orientation, race, gender, or how they were exposed to the virus—is part of the general population."
- *High-risk groups*—This term carries the threat of discrimination. It implies that certain people are at higher risk for AIDS merely by being members of some demographic group: homosexuals, Haitians, IV drug users, African Americans, and so on. In fact, no one in these groups or any other is automatically at higher risk for AIDS. The crucial variable is not "high-risk groups," but high-risk behavior—behavior that exposes someone to the virus.
- *AIDS victims*—Using this phrase works a kind of dark magic. It subtly suggests the people we care for—and perhaps we ourselves— are victims. The mere mention of that word carries with it images of the passive, helpless, long-suffering hospital patient, biding time until death. This is not an image that promotes health for people with AIDS or for effective caregiving. If it is unwise to refer to "cancer victims" or "heart disease victims," then surely it is unwise to use that term in speaking of people with AIDS.
- *AIDS virus versus AIDS*—Here we confront one of the most widespread confusions about AIDS. Far too many people confuse exposure to HIV with actually developing AIDS. In fact, there is no such thing as the

"AIDS virus." There is only HIV, which may — or may not — lead to AIDS.

- *Condoms* — We've heard many times that condoms are an essential part of safer sex. What's often glossed over is another fact: not all condoms are created equal. Those made from natural lamb skin do not prevent transmission of HIV. Latex condoms used with a spermicide (Nonoxynal-9) and water-soluble jelly offer far better protection.
- *Intimate sexual contact* — Ask one hundred people what intimate sexual contact is, and you'll get a hundred different answers. For some it means casual kissing. For others it connotes only intercourse. What's not made clear with this term is that some forms of sexual contact — such as unprotected rectal sex — pose a greater chance of transmitting HIV than others.[2]

As caregivers, many of us have learned enough about AIDS to avoid these misconceptions and others. It's easy to forget, however, that the people close to us may still use these buzzwords in their working vocabulary about AIDS. Keeping this in mind can help us when deciding who will know that our loved one has AIDS. It can also help us disclose that fact in the most accurate way.

FINDING A RELIABLE SOURCE OF INFORMATION

Getting solid information and filtering out unreliable information is essential. Just as important is finding a reliable and personal source of information about AIDS. This often means choosing a doctor, nurse, or counselor who knows the current research on AIDS. It also means finding someone who is sensitive to the emotional issues raised by AIDS. And as caregivers, we can look especially for a doctor who acknowledges our needs as well as the needs of those for whom we care.

Though a relationship with a doctor or other health professional is crucial, there's a potential problem with it too: being too attached and dependent. Some people with AIDS and their caregivers become troubled when they become too attached to their health care provider. It's important to find someone who will act as a "backup" for this person— someone who can answer questions or offer counseling when their regular provider is unavailable.

Professionals qualified to provide care for AIDS are hard to find and in great demand. It helps to have realistic expectations of them and their time. As caregivers, we can list reasonable questions before a medical visit—something that may lead to less frustration for all concerned.

What are other criteria for finding a good source of AIDS information? In general, they're the same as the criteria for selecting any effective doctor, nurse, therapist, or counselor:

- People who are open, honest, and available.
- People who recognize the limits of our knowledge about AIDS.
- People who acknowledge personal limits and are not afraid to be wrong and admit it.

In short, the qualities of a good provider are the same as those of a good caregiver. The provider, in fact, is often a *caregiver for you, the caregiver.* Remembering this can guide you in choosing a person you'll learn to trust.

BEYOND LEARNING—THE NEXT STEPS

As we adjust to the fact of AIDS in our life, we strive to find a center. By "center," we mean a source of strength, an inner resilience, something that can withstand the swiftly changing events in our life. It seems that AIDS has rendered everything in our life uncertain, and sometimes finding a center feels like huddling for safety in the eye of a hurricane.

For a time, gathering facts about AIDS may give us a framework for finding our center. Soon, however, it comes time for another question: "Given what we've learned, now how shall we live?" We have the facts; now how do we respond? Facts alone will not buy us serenity. Learning alone cannot silence the sadness, fear, shock, and other powerful Stage One emotions. Nor can learning by itself guarantee the most effective action in responding to AIDS.

So the center is elusive. And still we search for it. The message of this book is that we as caregivers can find our center. One key to doing so is learning, which is the subject of this chapter. In addition, however, two further steps are needed. One is working with feelings—a different kind of learning, one that turns us inward. This knowledge helps us get a handle on our emotions, allowing us to act effectively and to move toward acceptance. We will expand on this in Chapter Eight. Another step is taking effective action, the subject of Chapter Nine.

With these resources, we can discover a source of strength and serenity—one that can withstand the turbulence of caring for someone with AIDS. Ultimately, we can even speak of caregiving and acceptance. In Chapter Ten, we explain how.

CHAPTER 8

Phase B —
Working with Feelings

Millie was getting angrier and angrier. She resented Charlie for leaving her alone with the financial entanglements and for making her fend for herself without the least instruction.

She also became furious with him for cheating, and with herself for being such a sap. For two days she locked herself in her home and drew all the draperies, refusing to answer the telephone or door. She was hoarse from shouting. She ached from pounding on the bedding, the kitchen counter, and the sofa. For emotional comfort, she tried some drinks. But after two vodkas she felt sick. How could my Charlie have found comfort in M&M's — *Miltowns and martinis* — for so long? *she wondered.*

After two and a half days of calling her mother without getting an answer, Charlene went to Millie's house, fearing the worst. She knocked. There was no answer. So she let herself in, only to find Millie sitting cross-legged on the bathroom floor, staring at the wall.

Charlene helped her mother up. Millie began to wail and shudder, falling into her daughter's arms. It was almost an hour later when Millie seemed to finally run out of tears. Arm in arm with her daughter, she offered Charlene a cup of tea and some three-day-old homemade pecan pie. And over the pie and the tea, they talked about it all: Millie's loneliness, her feelings of ineptitude, her resentment toward Charlie, and her bitter anger toward Charlene and Odell for the pain they'd caused during Charlie's illness.

Charlene stayed with her mother. She left only after Millie dozed off in bed, exhausted from the ordeal.

* * * * *

For Mark, living with Phyllis for a few days during Dan's hospitalization was something Dan would call "anal excruciation—a pain in the ass." If she wasn't rearranging the furniture in their home, she was making everyone in the hospital miserable. She'd sweep into the nurses' station and interrogate the doctors. If she was in one of her copperhead moods, she'd "report" the nurses to the doctors and supervisors.

After five days, Mark, Phyllis, and the hospital staff had a meeting to call a truce. Mark joined with the others, telling Phyllis he knew what she was going through. Still, Mark continued, things would be easier for everyone if Phyllis would settle down. She needed to disarm the verbal grenades, listen to advice, and express her feelings in more positive ways.

It was all difficult for someone like Phyllis. She was sure of her competence—as sure that her son would flourish under her care as that her cakes would rise. She, a stranger to weakness, had no experience in working with feelings. But on this day, everything finally got to her. And when Mark met Phyllis's bright and contentious eyes, he saw tears. Phyllis, for the first time, was expressing emotions other than anger.

* * * * *

It seemed that Carmen was a changed woman when she brought little Xavier home from the hospital. For her the past six weeks had been grueling, and having her old boyfriend Xavier around only complicated her life. Even so, she was no longer confused. That man was now history. Her children were first and foremost. She realized for the first time that she wanted to enjoy them, to start bringing them some happiness.

Carmen told Yolanda how hard it had been, seeing little Xavier so sick. "I can handle my own sickness," she said, "but I cannot bear the baby being sick again." The guilt over her neglect, and what was worse, her shame over "causing" the baby's illness was more than she could stomach. And, for the first time, Carmen told both Yolanda and Inez how she felt to have such kind and loyal helpers.

Yolanda, Inez, and Carmen all hugged and cried. Hermenia remained stoic, distant. Perhaps she was too old and had been through too many wars with Carmen to really believe Carmen was changing.

* * * * *

As we saw in looking at the stages of our journey, caregiving arouses strong emotions. Those emotions cover the whole range of feeling, everything from sadness and despair to joy and intimacy. As caregivers, we may often say that our emotions are much closer to the surface than they were before life with AIDS. We may cry and get upset and get angry more often. We may also experience positive emotions more acutely, such as joy, hope, and love for the person with AIDS.

When talking about feelings, we quickly reach the limits of language. Words, in fact, are too coarse a medium to capture the complexity and intensity of our inner life. Fear, grief, shock, affection, joy—these terms go only so far in describing the world of our heart. Such words are only approximate. They help, but they bring us up to a certain point before fading into obscurity. For this reason, people have invented other languages to investigate and share their internal lives with others, such as the languages of music, painting, dance, and poetry. Likewise, nonverbal communication and body language are our physical expression of emotion.

To work with feelings, though, we can go beyond even these languages. We have an even more powerful tool: attention. With refined attention, we can observe thoughts and body sensations. These are the core elements of feeling—the atoms and molecules of our emotions. When we break down our feelings into these simpler elements, we can work with them.

More specifically, we can loosen the grip of negative emotions such as fear, sadness, and self-pity. We can build up energy. And we can generate positive feelings such as clarity and compassion. In this chapter, we explore this in more detail.

OPENING OURSELVES TO FEELING

When we learn that someone we love has AIDS, the discovery forces a series of radical shifts in our life. Suddenly AIDS is no longer an abstract concept, a condition "out there" in the world affecting people we only read or hear about. Suddenly the disease is as real as the person we love. It's changing the person we love. It's changing us. And things will never be the same. Suddenly AIDS lives, breathes, and has a human face.

If our journey as caregivers follows the stages mapped out in Part Two of this book, then sadness, shock, anger, and despair can block us from proceeding. They can be the hurdles, potholes, and hidden curves on our path.

And yet negative feelings, as numbing and painful as they are, reaffirm for us a basic truth about human psychology. We're reminded that it's so easy to live in our heads, in the realm of knowledge, concepts, facts, figures, and statistics. In social gatherings, some of us who know a lot about AIDS can offer cogent explanations of the condition. We can sum up the latest research, the current state of knowledge, and the status of the most recent experimental drug. We can talk glibly about current treatments and alternative therapies. Even so, it only takes one fact to cut through all this: Someone we love has AIDS. With this single fact, we're catapulted out of our rational mind. We're face-to-face again with a basic, primitive level of our psyche: the realm of pure feeling. This is the place that knows only pain and pleasure, satisfaction and suffering.

It's here that the wellsprings of our actions lie — not in our head, not in the intellect that analyzes, compares, computes, and plans. And it's with feelings that we enter our second phase of coming to terms with AIDS.

COMING TO TERMS WITH THE CHILD WITHIN

Some people have called the feeling part of ourselves the "child within." This child-like part of ourselves houses a rich world. It's here that we discover our abilities to create, play, explore, and laugh.

And it may also be a storehouse of negative feelings. Therapist Thomas Harris, M.D., explains:

> *Since the little person has no vocabulary during the most critical of his early experiences, most of his reactions are feelings. . . . He is small, he is dependent, he is inept, he is clumsy, he has no words with which to construct meanings. Emerson said we "must know how to estimate a sour look." The child does not know how to do this. A sour look turned in his direction can only produce feelings that add to his reservoir of negative data about himself.* It's my fault. Again. Always is. Ever will be. World without end.[1]

What's more, the child within reacts in extremes. It can seldom see the world with subtle gradations of feeling. Instead, the child classifies events into two broad and rigid categories:

This is terrible and *This is wonderful.* This view accounts for the intensity of many negative emotions we feel as caregivers.

In Stage One, we focus on discovery, the moment we learned that someone we love has AIDS. As we saw, that event cuts right to the level of pure feeling. Anger, shock, sadness, withdrawal, shame, and guilt—each of them may rise to the surface. We're immersed in the realm of feeling, in the child within. And when we discover someone we love has AIDS, the child within is wounded.

When people find out that our loved one has AIDS, we may glimpse their "child" too. Immediately we sense their discomfort. They're tense, uncomfortable. They grope for words. They can't bear the awkward silence. They want to say something—anything —to smooth things over, to make things somehow right again.

Many of our friends truly care. Yet in their fumbling for a response, what may emerge are platitudes. We want the profound insight, the secret answer, the hidden knowledge that will make our loved one well again. We want to restore our former life, to exchange realities, if only for a moment. At the very least, we want to stop hurting for a little while. Instead, the words people offer seem like the sentiments of a greeting card: brittle, hollow, beside the point.

Though emotional support from others is crucial, we can learn powerful ways to work with our own feelings. That's the key concern in this chapter.

SEEING INTO THE CAREGIVER'S HEART

As caregivers, we may wake each day with a crushing, overwhelming complex of emotions. The first step in our journey is to separate out the strands of these feelings. These emotions have a pattern, an "anatomy." By understanding the anatomy of our feelings, we can see more directly into our own heart.

By looking inside, we can gain some perspective and mastery over our feelings. Doing so cannot only reduce our pain—it can make us caregivers with more energy and compassion.

There's freedom in awareness. Feelings come to us in waves of thoughts and body sensations, and we can learn to recognize the waves associated with a particular feeling. That's awareness—the first step to becoming effective caregivers. When we pour awareness on to a negative emotion, we begin on sure ground.

There's power in naming. Even the most devastating anxiety can be reduced by naming it and describing it. By naming feelings, we can start to detach from them, to stand outside them. When we do—even if only for a few seconds—we're less overwhelmed. In that moment, we're no longer in the grip of that emotion, no longer driven by it or controlled by it. Giving grief a name may rescue us from feeling like we're going crazy. Giving anger a name may enable us to let go of overpowering rage.

That's the first of our goals: learning to name, describe, recognize, and become aware of feelings associated with caregiving. As a second goal, we encourage identifying with others. The feelings we have are shared by many caregivers. No two people will have the same experience. Still, there are other people on the caregiving path. By identifying with others, we can feel less alone, less isolated, less unique.

Why is it important to work with feelings—especially the negative emotions that commonly arise around the diagnosis of AIDS? For one, negative emotions drain our vital energy. This is nothing mysterious. In fact, you can observe it directly. Observe people who are constantly in a negative emotional state. Like Millie, they are dominated by sadness, self-pity, anger, despair, or fear. Often these people are also low on energy. They complain of feeling tired, listless, or apathetic. Even people in a balanced, basically positive emotional state feel drained simply by being around a negative person.

If we learn how to work with negative feelings, an empowering event occurs: We feel stronger, lighter, clearer. We have more energy for daily tasks.

This is especially important for caregivers. The most frequent complaint about caring for anyone with a chronic illness is about lacking energy. "It takes so much out of me," says Yolanda. "I'm beat. I just feel drained at the end of the day."

Mark says, "Sometimes it's just so much work to face Dan's illness after a long hard day at the office. It takes all my energy."

That's why work with emotions is so important: it can unleash the energy needed for caregiving.

THE NATURE OF FEELINGS

Understanding our feelings—where they come from, how to describe them, how they interact, how they change—is crucial. But in itself, this may not be enough. Effective caregiving in this phase requires us to figure out how to cope with this daily barrage of emotion.

Part of the difficulty arises from something we've referred to before: the complex, wave-like nature of feelings. They seem to arise, wash over us, and then subside, like the tide. Then they recur, swirling around us again. Also, the texture of these feelings changes constantly: sometimes sadness, pity, shame, and exhaustion; at other times anger, shock, even aggression. They mix in volatile ways that can make us feel like exploding.

How emotions arise depends on the circumstances, mirroring the shifting nature of addiction and HIV disease. "On the day Dan got diagnosed," says Mark, "after the shock subsided, I felt overwhelming sadness and fear."

"The night before, Carmen shot up," says Yolanda. "I felt furious and then guilty. How could I be mad at a sick person? What if she died before I woke up?"

"One day Dan seems fine," says Mark at a support group meeting. "I forget about caregiving for a while and, we just exist as lovers, friends. Twenty-four hours later, he seems worse—more fatigued, more irritable, more confused—and there's no clear reason why. I end up feeling out of control, powerless."

Feelings ebb and flow depending on what's happening in our life. To some extent the anxiety or sadness is always there; it accompanies us wherever we go, whatever we do. Anyone who has lived with chemical dependency knows firsthand about chronic anxiety, sadness, and powerlessness over such emotions.

The reality of Phase B is that some days, or some parts of the day, we feel better. Other times we feel worse. And often, feelings change from better to worse without warning. Something our loved one does or says does not necessarily mire us in depression or sadness. Sometimes it's just what's going on with us that leads to the shifting, uncontrollable, murky, quicksand-like nature of feeling.

NEGATIVE WAYS OF COPING WITH FEELINGS

In Phase B we confront the question of how to cope with emotion. Some ways of coping work well. Others work for a short time but not so well in the long run. Among the less effective are these:

- *Sacrificing our own health*—not taking proper care of ourselves: doing too much and not getting enough rest; eating too much or too little; showing the symptoms of illness; getting sick more often than we used to; getting an ulcer, headache, or other stress-related condition.
- *Using chemicals*—drinking or using other drugs to forget about it all (if we're chemically dependent, this may mean relapsing): abusing Valium, Xanax, or sleeping pills, or smoking or drinking lots of coffee.

- *Displacing feelings, especially anger*—losing our temper: exploding over minor irritations; directing anger at innocent bystanders; kicking the dog; yelling in traffic; taking it out on co-workers, customers, friends, and other people we care for, then feeling guilty.
- *Withdrawing*—removing ourselves physically or emotionally from our loved ones or from any source of conflict: spending more time away from home; isolating ourselves to avoid situations that cause distress and not talking about it; refusing to take part in conversations even when we're physically present, or refusing to take part with any feeling.
- *Negative denial*—refusing to admit there is any problem: pretending that things have just gone wrong temporarily; maintaining that we're really in control, that we can turn the situation around at anytime if we really want to; feeling like we can make people do what we want them to.

Denial is a shifting and subtle feeling. It may control us when we're least aware of it. We can even use caregiving itself to shut out the awareness of feeling. This happens to Mark: "There are days when I don't want any time by myself. I want to focus only on Dan—how he feels, what he needs, what he's doing. That way I don't have to deal with the fear I feel."

Note that this kind of denial is not the same as *choosing* to focus on something other than AIDS. When we make that choice, we're still, on some level, aware of feeling pain, sadness, shame, or fear. We simply observe the feeling, acknowledge it, and opt to leave it behind for now. Negative denial is automatic and unconscious. And it can be dangerous. We end up stuffing feelings without knowing we're doing so. There's no awareness or choice involved.

"Becoming numb to feeling" or "repressing emotions" are other words for negative denial. As Timmen Cermak, M.D., points out, one way to respond to an intolerable barrage of emotions is to not feel them. We try to shield ourselves against them. We try at all possible costs to make sure they don't come to the surface, saying we don't really care anymore, that none of it really matters. This almost means pretending that the feelings don't exist. People who are good at this may even believe the pretense after awhile.

The following methods of coping are *dysfunctional.*

- *Enabling*—allowing or encouraging our loved ones to feel self-pity, give up, become codependent, or take advantage of us. By doing these things, we actually foster negative emotion and codependence in the people we care for.
- *Acting as a codependent*—tying our sense of well-being directly to our loved one's. If the person we're caring for is okay, then we're fine. But if he or she is sick, fatigued, or angry, our serenity is shot.

Dysfunctional ways of coping simply means they don't work very well. They don't do the job. On the surface they seem to help, at least at first. After all, these ways of coping let us get on with life for a time. But the anxiety, fear, and grief are still there; the time to work through them is just being postponed. We use a ton of energy to keep the lid on. If we're not aware of these feelings, they may surface when we least expect them. In the process, we sometimes lose control and blow off steam like a pressure cooker—or explode.

Coping methods are ineffective when they dominate us without our knowledge. Then they keep us from the feelings we need to know about.

> *Millie screams at another driver during a traffic jam. The underlying reasons are that she's tired, feeling sick, and anxious about Charlie and the future. But she experiences only her anger.*

> *Inez suffers headaches whenever she's upset about her mom, her little brother, and her own fate. She knows little of her internal pain—fear, grief, loneliness —since she's converted them into a headache. Without help, she may suffer from headaches the rest of her life.*

> *Mark tells us, "When Dan's okay, I'm okay." On the surface, that seems logical. But the fact is that Dan has AIDS. It's likely he'll feel sick much of the time. And that may bar Mark from feeling well most of the time too.*

Reacting in such unhealthy ways is one way of responding to the endless tides of feeling that wash over us. One feeling blends into another: Anger masks fear or sadness; shock obscures the pain. What's more, the mind tries to "protect" us from the feelings it judges we can't handle. It enlists dysfunctional behaviors—even though they eventually turn against us. We still have to face the feelings, but now with interest added.

POSITIVE WAYS OF COPING WITH FEELINGS

There are alternatives—positive ways to cope with feelings. These positive methods are related to the negative, ineffective ways. Sometimes they may even feel the same. That's because each coping method exists on a continuum: on one end, unhealthy, ineffective, and dysfunctional; on the other end, healthy, effective, and functional.

With AIDS, we can admit that we are powerless over our loved one's illness. Then we are able to proceed by looking at ourselves and how we are to function with this illness in our lives. We, the caregivers, need to be fully responsible for ourselves first. Then we can provide care more effectively.

Feelings have "seasons" of their own. We can learn to acknowledge the seasons of feelings, the rhythms of activity and passivity, of joy and sorrow, fear and calm—the wave-like nature of our feelings. Understanding this is one step toward coping with negative emotion.

In caregiving, we experience the full cycle of emotions. As we work with the feelings involved, we have a couple of aims: (1) to remain alert to what is happening to reduce the element of surprise, and (2) to explain the past and and to better understand what's happening to us right now. By admitting and keeping tabs on our feelings, we have a better chance of coping effectively. By understanding ourselves better, we have a better chance of keeping things in perspective.

We'll frame our discussion of healthy Phase B coping styles by using some slogans. These slogans are central to Twelve Step programs such as Alcoholics Anonymous.

One Day at a Time

This slogan reminds us about positive denial. We don't have to constantly remember that the people we love have HIV infection or AIDS. One of the most powerful things we can do is focus on whatever is happening today: work, reading, recreation, the arts, plans for dinner, or simply watching television. This is living in the moment, something that helps us as caregivers. To live in the moment means seeing that the people we care for are *not dying today*. They are here with us, and that is enough. This is living with AIDS one day at a time.

If we carry rigid expectations for the future, living one day at a time will be impossible. The alternative is to replace *expectations* with *expectancies*. For example, take the way Millie responds to the question, "How are you?" She might assume there's only one honest answer: "I'm doing fine. I expected to feel positive and filled with energy today. And I do." To Millie, feeling any sadness or loss of energy means she's failed to meet her expectation. In that case, "I feel fine" is a lie.

But what if she softened her expectation into an expectancy? Then she could say this: "Well, Charlie's talking and thinking clearly, and I'm out of bed. I'm kind of sad, and I'd hoped to have more energy. But for today I can acknowledge where I am and it's okay. Tomorrow the sun will rise and I'll awaken again with *some* energy to carry on the day."

Expectations are rigid agendas for how we'll feel and what we'll get done in one day, one year, or one lifetime. It means we face the world with a list of ultimatums, a litany of requirements. And in doing so, we write an emotional check for disappointment, frustration, and unmet goals. There's no way any of us can measure up. Including AIDS in the picture makes rigid expectations even more likely to go unmet.

In contrast, an expectancy provides for a realistic sense of what's to come. It offers the general outlook, the big picture. It's based not on having, not on doing, but on *being*. After ten years of caregiving, we may not have the sizable savings account we'd expected. We may not have the income, the car, or the house we'd dreamed of. And we may have to cancel this trip or that vacation.

Instead, we can function more comfortably. We can jettison these expectations and nurture expectancy. "Even though things have changed in ways I never dreamed," says Mark, "I've lived each day with gratitude. I've learned. I've worked with my feelings. And I've done everything I knew how to do." With this comes the potential—not for perfect satisfaction—but for serenity.

Making plans for the future is always healthy. Instead of waiting for the people we love to die, we can get on with life. To be totally without goals leads us toward the other extreme: passivity and hopelessness. To meet unmet goals is what, for some, keeps life interesting and worthwhile.

Still, any plan is only as workable as it is flexible. If our plan gives us only two alternatives—meet the expectation or despair—then we've wrapped ourselves in chains. Buoying ourselves with expectancy helps us live today with joy.

When caregivers become obsessed with AIDS, they may feel paralyzed with sadness and shock. Some even long for suicide: "Things will end soon anyway," says Millie. "Better to feel nothing than to feel this bad." The alternative is to seize the day. Suppose it's true that time with the person we love is limited. Then why throw away today? Pessimism may be a more realistic view of life, but optimism may help us live longer.

Easy Does It

If we lived constantly with the full emotional impact of all the Stage One feelings, we'd be stuck, lost, overwhelmed. It can be disabling to be aware of them at all times. When caring for a person with AIDS, we can loosen the grip these emotions have on us. We can choose to go easier on ourselves and on others.

Live and Let Live

As human beings we sometimes need to be alone. As caregivers, we need to be with people other than the one we care for. In other words, we need to live. That means withdrawing from caregiving occasionally—to write, meditate, pray, listen to music, do our own work, see friends, or simply relax.

Our loved ones, too, need space to be alone. In other words, we need to let them live. Fostering their self-reliance can help them overcome feelings of powerlessness and dependency. We can grant others the right to go about their business as we proceed with ours. Respecting their need to be separate will reinforce the healthy bonding that exists in our relationships. That kind of respect also helps us grow toward interdependence.

It's healthy to live and let live.

But for the Grace of God, Go I

"Let's face it: Dan is sick, not you." This is what Mark's friend Sherman says when Mark calls with an attack of the "guilts." "This fact may not please you, but it's reality. And there's no need for you to feel shame or guilt about it."

We have a right to take care of ourselves, to enjoy our own health, to promote it and be grateful for it. We can stay well. As healthy caregivers, we'll be better equipped to care when needed. And we're not needed twenty-four hours each day.

Get a Sponsor

In AA, a sponsor is another alcoholic who has been attending group meetings for some time, someone actively living the Twelve Steps as a means to recovery. Newcomers to an AA group are encouraged to find one of these more experienced members to act as their guide or advisor.

When caring for someone with AIDS, we recommend adopting a kind of sponsor or "buddy." We can seek out special friends whom we trust, people who will understand and listen. Doing so will help overcome the isolation and loneliness that come with the role of an AIDS caregiver.

Many AIDS organizations provide buddies for people with AIDS and their caregivers. Finding a buddy whose experience parallels ours can be the most effective way to choose one. Learning from that person's experience alleviates the feeling that "no one understands." It proves to us that we are not alone.

Let Go and Let God

Contact with a Power greater than ourselves is a touchstone in the face of uncertainty or possible death. Many work to ensure that contact: going to extra meetings, seeing a sponsor or spiritual advisor daily, meditating, staying aware of their spiritual condition, and reading appropriate materials. Ultimately we are not in control of our loved ones or their illness. For that reason, having a spiritual center becomes even more important.

For some of us, the words *God* or *Higher Power* are a stumbling block in living out this slogan. This need not be. *Any* source of energy and strength in our life can be our Higher Power for today. And that can range from the pages of a book or the loving touch of a friend to the smile of a child. "Let God" means opening ourselves up to help wherever it meets us and not relying soley on our own self-will.

* * * * *

Each of these slogans leads us to a positive coping method. And, as AA reminds us, we'll need to exert energy and take action to fully benefit from these positive coping styles. We'll discuss action more in Phase C.

Positive coping styles empower us because they involve choice:

> *"I'm getting angry at Odell and Charlene, and I choose to not deal with it right now," says Millie. "Rather than being alone and isolating from Charlie, I'll take some time later to call a friend who will understand. I'll talk about how I feel, and if I cry that's okay too. For now, I'll just sit with my husband for a while."*

> *"I can see that drinking or drugging won't make anything better," says Yolanda. "In fact, they'll just make things worse. God help me stay clean today. If I can't make it through the crisis, how will Carmen? I choose to not use. Instead, I'll go to another NA meeting and talk to my sponsor."*

> *"I know I'm sad," says Carmen. "But my little Inez is fine today, and I want to enjoy her. I'll let go of the sadness for now and focus on the joy of being with her. Let's go for a walk, Cara."*

> *Mark sees Kaposi's sarcoma on Dan's leg; he looks up at Dan's smiling face and curly hair. I'm grateful that he's*

here today, *Mark thinks,* and I love him. That's what counts. I choose to forget being angry over our disagreements. I want to enjoy him now.

> *Millie breaks down and sobs over some character's fate in a soap opera. "I feel so strange," she says. "It's only a silly TV show. Why am I crying so hard?" Instead of feeling shock over her reaction, Millie can unravel that feeling. She can ask, "What am I really sad about?" And when she does, Millie discovers what's at the bottom of it: her powerlessness over Charlie's AIDS combined with frustration at her sense of loss. After the next commercial, she decides to change her environment. She leaves the house for a trip to the store.*

As we noted earlier in this chapter, awareness—knowing what we're feeling—is crucial. Our key slogan is: "It's okay to feel the feelings." The truth is that we can fully experience our feelings and still survive. In fact, awareness of these feelings is what frees us to make choices.

As we work with feelings, our purpose is twofold: (1) to bring these choices we can make to our awareness, and (2) to deepen our skill at making them. These choices really grow out of a larger affirmation: saying yes to life. Perry Tilleraas, in *The Color of Light: Daily Meditations for All of Us Living with AIDS,* quotes Graham, a person with AIDS:

> *I realize that this diagnosis of AIDS presents me with a choice: the choice either to be a hopeless victim and die of AIDS, or to make my life right now what it always ought to have been.*[2]

UNDERSTANDING THE DYNAMICS OF FEELINGS

Before talking about another positive coping method, let's take a deeper look at the nature of feelings.

When people speak about their feelings, they commonly speak about the *objects* of their feelings. Suppose, for example, we asked Millie to describe her greatest fear. She'd respond, "Losing Charlie to complications resulting from AIDS, having to live out the rest of my life alone, or discovering one day that I too have AIDS.

Each of Millie's responses points to objects of fear: being alone, seeing her husband die, getting sick herself. But what about the *dynamics* of her fear? Could she describe them? She might be puzzled by the question. And in that respect, she's like many of us.

When we speak of the dynamics of a feeling, we're viewing feelings in a different way. We are not asking about objects— what we're afraid *of*. In contrast, we're asking what happens inside us when this feeling takes us over. The question is not "What are you afraid of?" Instead, it's "What does the *experience* of fear feel like to you? What happens in your body and mind when you feel fear, sadness, anxiety, or any other Stage One emotion?" When we ask the latter questions, we're talking about the dynamics of feeling.

As caregivers for people with AIDS, this is a crucial point for us in Phase B. Both the caregiver and the person with AIDS will experience powerful feelings through all stages of the journey described in Part Two of this book. The *objects* of those feelings may be the same for both people. For example, both Mark and Dan feel anxiety over losing friends and telling their parents about AIDS.

However, the objects of their feelings may differ. Charlie feels the most anxiety over the threat of death. In contrast, Millie worries most about whether to leave Charlie. And she wonders if it will ever be safe to have sex again; Charlie could care less. Yolanda is afraid that Carmen will go back to Xavier, while Carmen's biggest fear is being alone.

So the person with AIDS and the caregiver are immersed in feelings. Some objects of those feelings are the same for both of them; others are different. But when we shift our view to the dynamics of feeling, we discover that even though the objects of a feeling may differ, the dynamics of that feeling are similar. We and our loved ones may feel sadness, anger, guilt, or shame toward different objects. Yet the dynamics of sadness, anger, guilt, or shame can be the same for many of us. Throughout the journey of caregiving, we can talk of a real union with our loved ones at the level of feeling, the level of the heart.

The Three Elements of Feeling

Since the 1960s we've been flooded with self-help books, tapes, and seminars. Throughout them all reverberates a slogan: "To feel better, get in touch with your feelings." As caregivers, we may hear this bit of advice constantly and grow tired of it.

While this is a sound idea, the books and speakers often leave us confused about exactly what this means. How, exactly, do we get in touch with feelings? And just what *are* feelings, anyway? One answer is to look at two levels of any feeling: the object and the dynamic. This approach is drawn from the tradition of Buddhist insight meditation, as well as other Eastern traditions.

Earlier in this chapter we mentioned that feelings come in waves. And as caregivers, we may feel powerless over the gales of fear, sadness, guilt, and shame that wash over us. Once we see the nature of those waves more precisely, though, we discover a powerful method of responding to feeling. Simply put, feelings come in three parts: (1) thoughts, (2) sensations in the body, and (3) reactions. These are three main threads in the dynamic of any feeling. We can observe these threads in great detail—without judging them. When that happens, we find that negative emotions start to loosen their grip on us.

Take one feeling common to caregivers: fear. This feeling arises in each of us with specific thoughts—"mind sensations." Each of us has our own list of thoughts tied to certain emotions. For example, we might imagine the person we care for in a hospital bed, dying from pneumonia. Along with these thoughts comes a stream of words and judgments: "My God, he's dying. How terrible! This is the worst possible thing that could happen. What if it does?" These are thoughts: words and pictures occurring in the mind. This is the first element of feeling.

Tied to these thoughts will be sensations in the body—the second element of feeling. And with a little practice, we can pinpoint them more exactly: pounding in the heart, tightness in the chest, a crampy feeling in the pit of the stomach, sweatiness of the palms. With the experience of fear, we may detect these sensations and many more. In working with feelings, it helps greatly to identify and become familiar with our "stockpile" of body sensations.

In our most difficult moments, sensations pound through us like an avalanche. And in those moments, we're often tempted to do one thing: React. Resist. It's common to do something—anything—that will put a lid on that explosive brew of thoughts and sensations: deny feelings, repress or "stuff" feelings, sleep twelve hours each day, overeat, drink or use other drugs—anything to numb the pain. Such reactions are the third element of feeling.

All of these tactics are attempts to beat feelings into submission—examples of the negative coping methods we looked at earlier. They are knee-jerk reactions to unpleasant sensations. And because they're automatic, these reactions give us no choice. In fact, these negative methods rob us of choice.

Thoughts, body sensations, and reactions—here we find the key elements of any feeling. Each time we feel any emotion, pleasant or unpleasant, thoughts ripple through our minds and sensations course through our bodies. Then we react. All the names we give to feelings—fear, pleasure, sadness, shock, anxiety, joy—are just labels for varied mixtures of these elements.

LEARNING TO ACKNOWLEDGE
AND OBSERVE FEELINGS

As mentioned earlier, the most common way to respond to a negative feeling is to resist it. And people have a number of strategies for doing so. The problem is that many strategies are like trying to put out a kitchen fire with grease: they just feed the flames while the fire rages beyond control.

As we become more skilled at working with emotions, we start to grasp a subtle fact: Much of our suffering comes not from the negative feeling itself. It comes from our futile efforts to *resist* or react to the feeling. If the thoughts and sensations could flow through us, unblocked and without resistance, then we could be done with the feeling for the moment. We could let the feelings go.

Instead, we "lock" around feelings. We repress, stuff, deny, block, resist. Without locking, troubling thoughts and sensations could move through us, over us, and out of us without leaving a residue—like water off a duck's back. When we lock around feelings, however, the thoughts and sensations turn into something hard, solid, brittle, and painful.

Here we can use another homegrown analogy. Resisting feelings is like trying to keep a pot of water from boiling over on the stove. One strategy is to keep forcing the lid on, tighter and tighter. Unfortunately, this only raises the temperature inside the pot. Even if we keep shoving on the lid, the pot is still getting ready to explode.

Instead of forcing the lid, however, we could try two other strategies: First, turn down the flame under the pot. Next, open the lid and see exactly what's in the pot. Both of these commonsense actions allow steam to escape, decreasing the pressure. They also suggest how we can reduce the suffering imposed by negative feelings.

Turning Down the Flame

What if we could experience feelings with less resistance? If we did, we'd simply let them come to awareness without trying to stuff or deny them. We'd simply open ourselves to the thoughts that come with them. We'd let their sensations wash over us without judging them. Instead of labeling the feeling as "terrible" or "disastrous," we'd simply acknowledge it. In the process, we change the third element of our feelings: resistance or reaction.

It's okay to just "feel the feeling." It's okay to let feelings be what they are. Doing so is like turning down the flame under the pot. When we stop resisting negative feelings, they often stop boiling over. Those feelings start running out of gas. They lose their energy, their power, their grip over us. Acknowledging the feeling removes one of the three elements of negative feelings—resistance. And that's why acknowledgment goes a long way toward freeing us from these negative feelings.

Acknowledging feelings means we stop fighting back the wave of emotion. Instead, we'd let the wave of feeling rise, wash over us, and flow back to sea. Doing this is not always pleasant. In fact, opening up to feeling may bring real discomfort. But there's a difference between discomfort and suffering. Discomfort is temporary; it passes. Only when we resist it does the discomfort turn into suffering.

Opening the Lid and Seeing Exactly What's in the Pot

Beyond turning down the flame, we can take one more step: open the lid and see what's in the pot. That is, we can look to see exactly what *thoughts* and what *sensations* make up the feeling we're experiencing.

As an example, take a feeling we may often experience as caregivers—*sadness*. Sadness, like any other feeling, is a mixture of thoughts running through the mind and sensations rippling through the body.

To work effectively with sadness, we can first turn down the flame on this feeling—that is, acknowledge it. In addition, we can observe exactly what thoughts come with it. We can notice the images, mental pictures, and words that make up those thoughts. What's more, we can observe the sensations we're experiencing. We can describe what they're like and see exactly *where* in the body they are occurring. For example, Mark, observing his experience of sadness, describes it this way:

> *When I'm sad, the same images run through my mind, kind of like a bad dream. I see myself alone in our big house without Dan. All Dan's things are scattered around—his clothes, his books, his records, photos of him with our cats. But Dan is gone. I hear myself asking him to come downstairs, to pick up his stuff, to straighten up. Then I realize— again—that he's died; he's gone.*
>
> *Then, while this picture is running in my mind, a real feeling of isolation and despair washes over me. I start to feel clammy. My hands and fingertips feel like they're getting cold. My feet start to prickle with sensation, kind of like going numb. I see myself wanting to wrap my arms around myself, bury myself in a blanket, and curl up into a ball. I want to get drunk. I want to retreat, to hide from the loneliness.*

Here Mark demonstrates everything we've said about working with feeling. First, he *acknowledged* the sadness— enough, anyway, to let his thoughts and sensations come to awareness. Next, he *observed* the thoughts and sensations precisely. He was able to describe the mental pictures and words that come with his experience of sadness. What's more, he could tell what sensations he was feeling—coldness, numbness—and where in his body they were taking place.

Observing the thoughts and sensations in this way takes even more power away from the feeling.

With these two strategies—acknowledging and observing—we can start to take the heat off ourselves when a negative feeling arises. We can stop boiling over or caving in to the feeling. We can keep the temporary discomfort caused by the thoughts and sensations from turning into a solid wall of suffering.

OBSERVING FEELINGS

When we acknowledge and observe feelings, we may find ourselves in a new state of mind. That state has been called different names: "witness consciousness," "the witness self," "observer consciousness," and many more. We'll simply call it *observing.*

Many spiritual traditions in the world have handed down techniques for observing feelings. They come under a variety of names: yoga, reflection, contemplation, and many more. In Twelve Step groups, people speak of them as *prayer and meditation.* All of these techniques have one thing in common: They allow us to acknowledge the thoughts and sensations that make up our feelings without judging, denying, or reacting, and they allow us to directly observe those thoughts and sensations.

This does not involve anything mysterious. It simply means learning to name, observe, and experience. Doing so is a skill, much like the everyday skills of driving a car or playing the piano. We can accurately speak of working with feelings as a skill. And as a skill, we can learn it and practice it until it becomes second nature for us.

The fact is that every human being experiences fear, sadness, shock, and other feelings that caregivers feel. The problem is that most people don't gain skill at working with feelings as they grow older. They are just as powerless over fear or anxiety at age seventy as they are at age seven.

Opening to Feeling

We can turn this situation around. The advantages of gaining skill with feelings are many. As we observe and acknowledge feelings, we learn an essential fact: Feelings are not solid or permanent. They're permeable. They have spaces. They're evanescent; they arise and subside. They're especially intense at times; then they lift and we feel better. They don't last.

With practice, we can see this directly. Then, we go beyond the old adage, "This, too, shall pass." We're able to say, "This feeling is passing *right now.*" To say this is to feel more free in the midst of any emotion—even as we feel it.

Discovering What Helps

Observing feeling carries with it another potential gift: discovering *what actually helps.* When we're no longer seized by negative emotions, we can see our loved one's situation as it is. Our own fears, needs, desire for control, and requirements do not have to color our response. We can discover what our loved one needs right now, in this moment. We can let the most caring thought, word, or action arise in us and flow out of us spontaneously. That makes us better caregivers.

Ram Dass and Paul Gorman make this point in talking about the "witness self"—their term for observing:

> *The Witness, however, is not passive, complacent, or indifferent. Indeed, while it's not attached to a particular outcome, its presence turns out to bring about change. As we bring what is into the light of clear awareness, we begin to see that the universe is providing us with abundant clues as to the nature of the suffering before us, what is being asked, what fears have been inhibiting us, and, finally, what*

might really help. *All we have to do is listen—really listen.*[3]

We can apply this to daily events in caregiving. Dan wakes up in the middle of the night, despairing over AIDS, feeling its limits more acutely than usual. "Why me?" he asks, breaking the dark silence. "Why did I have to get sick? I feel like Job in the *Bible*—a test case for some new plague in the universe, a pawn in some cosmic gamble. I'm a guinea pig for every new drug and treatment," says Dan, his sarcasm melting into tears. "I feel like some lab rat racing through a maze. I want out," he sobs. "Count me out of this damn game. Why me? Why?"

Mark opens his eyes, knowing that he and Dan have been over this a hundred times. His first impulse is to give all his old answers: There's no one up there choosing who gets AIDS and who doesn't. We can see no design or grand purpose in people dying from AIDS; if there is, that purpose is bigger than we are. Sickness is part of living, and we don't know why. It's the same point made by the bumper sticker Dan pointed out one day: "Shit Happens."

As Dan talks, Mark goes through all this in his mind—again. For a few moments he's not even listening to Dan. Then as Mark wakes up, he lets go of his stream of thought. In fact, he stops rehearsing his responses and just listens. He hears Dan's tirade as if for the first time. And this time he detects something new: Dan is not really asking, "Why me?" Dan knows that Mark has no ultimate answer. Dan doesn't really want a *why*; he's asking for a *how*: "How am I going to make it through this? I don't know if I can make it. Maybe I can't."

Hearing this new shade of meaning, Mark responds. He finds himself hugging Dan, whispering, "It's okay. I'm here." Mark has discovered what Dan needed to feel: *I'm not alone, even if I am sick. I can count on someone.* Here the love flows through both of them as they hold each other. And for the moment, that is enough.

EXPRESSING FEELINGS

Acknowledging and observing feelings have one thing in common: They are events that take place inside us. They result from seeing into our own heart and mind. These means of observing, however, say little about another topic: letting others know what's going on inside us.

Simple logic tells us that we must breathe so as not to suffocate. The logic of ventilating feelings is just as simple—and just as urgent. Just as some chemical reactions can take place only in darkness, emotional poisons grow when we refuse to shine a light on our feelings. They become lodged in us like shards of glass in a bare foot.

As we open up to feelings, we may well feel pain. But we also discover a way through the pain. It hurts to remove those pieces of glass, but it also gives the foot a chance to heal. On the other side of resentment is love. On the other side of fear is calmness. When we express negative feelings, we release them. And when we free up the energy that goes into holding those feelings, we may find a surprising reservoir of strength.

This is a central issue for caregivers: We're subject to powerful feelings at every stage of our journey. And so are the people we care for—our loved ones with AIDS. To heal our relationships, we must be open. We need to not only observe and acknowledge our feelings; we need to let others into our hearts. That calls on us to express our feelings.

Like the phrase "get in touch with your feelings," the slogan "express your feelings" has received a lot of hype. But what exactly do we mean by "expressing feelings"? And can we speak of *skill* at expressing feelings—much as we've just spoken about skill at getting in touch with feelings?

Expressing feelings is a skill we can develop and practice.

And there's one key to learning and perfecting this skill: speaking in "I" messages versus "you" messages.

Imagine that Mark wants to spend an evening with friends and go to a party without Dan. Mark is feeling worn down from his role as Dan's caregiver and simply wants an evening away from home. The intention is not to end the relationship or compromise it in any way; the idea is simply to take a break.

Mark could express this wish to Dan in at least two different ways. We give an example of each:

1. "Living with you just wears me down sometimes. You make a lot of demands on me. After awhile, I just can't function without a break from you. Will you let me get away for just one night?"

2. "I care for you. And in order to keep feeling the way I do, I need a break sometimes. This evening out will help me a lot. I'll be back soon, okay?"

These two messages convey nearly the same content. Even so, they make entirely different statements about the relationship between Dan and Mark.

Message number one implies that Dan is demanding and exhausting to live with. It also hints at codependence—the idea that Mark needs Dan's "permission" to "get away for just one night." In short, the tone is accusing and blaming. The continual use of the word "you" makes it the verbal equivalent of pointing a finger at Dan.

For Mark, this way of expressing feelings merely invites a defensive, angry response from Dan. We can easily imagine what it might be: "I am *not* hard to live with. I do not make any demands of you. And anyway, I didn't ask to get AIDS. So your exhaustion isn't my fault. Just go out and do whatever the hell you want. You don't need my permission."

Message number two is a sharp contrast. Here Mark accuses Dan of nothing. Instead, Mark talks only about what *he* feels, what *he* wants, and what *he* needs. He doesn't imply in any way that Dan is making him feel run down or is making undue demands. Mark is merely stating how he views the situation, and he's not demanding that Dan agree.

What's more, message number two communicates caring, affection, and contact: "I'll be back soon, okay?" Here the focus is not on blaming or accusing, but on positive emotions that affirm Mark's relationship with Dan.

This example demonstrates the technique—and benefits—of expressing feelings as "I" messages. The basic idea when doing so is to talk about ourselves, not the people we care for. We can take responsibility for our observations, our feelings, our thoughts, and our wishes. And if we can follow the "I" message with a positive emotion, the message becomes even more powerful. As caregivers, these are skills we can cultivate every day in loving someone with AIDS.

* * * * *

Expressing feelings is a central path in our journey as caregivers. Discovering, adapting, coasting, and colliding—these are the broad outlines of our stories, the mileposts in our journey. Each of us will move through these stages in a unique way. And there's no need to do so alone. We can let others know how the trip is going. We can name, acknowledge, observe, and express what we feel.

SUMMING UP

We covered a lot of ground in this chapter on working with feelings. And most of it can be summed in a simple list of four steps. These are the keys to skillful work with feelings:

1. Name the Feeling

If you can, give the feeling a name—anger, sadness, shock. Don't worry about being precise or complete in your description of the feeling. That's not necessary. All that's needed is awareness that a feeling is starting to boil to the surface. Identifying the object and the dynamics of the feeling may help to give it a voice At this point, a quick mental note will be enough to shift us into the role of observer.

2. Acknowledge the Feeling

Instead of suppressing the feeling, let it rise to the surface. When we stuff negative feelings, we give them more energy. The healing alternative is to acknowledge the feeling. Our aim is to let go of all judgments and evaluations. Anger, sadness, guilt, shock, shame—feelings that arise in us are neither good nor bad. They simply *are.* It's fine to just feel the feelings. They just happen. Our most useful focus is not on what *should be;* rather, it's on *what is.*

3. Observe the Feeling

When a strong feeling surfaces, we can remind ourselves to simply observe it. We can notice the thoughts, body sensations, and reactions that come with it. This is the most empowering way to ride the crests of those waves of feeling. And with the ability to observe comes the ability to control.

All this is another way of saying one thing: Instead of denying or blocking the feeling, embrace it. *Love* the feeling. Loving the feeling does not call on us to wallow in it or take masochistic delight in suffering. Instead, it means acknowledging the feeling without judgment and getting to know it well.

4. Express the Feeling

We can focus on stating what we think, feel, and want. At the same time, we avoid accusing, blaming, or demanding that the other person acknowledge our viewpoint.

* * * * *

With these strategies, we gain an empowering way to work with our feelings. This can serve us at any stage of the caregiving journey. Even so, work with feelings in Phase B is not the only tool we can use on the journey to acceptance. Besides making contact with our inner world, we can face the world outside us. We can change our world in some way that heals us. And doing so means moving into Phase C: taking action.

CHAPTER 9

Phase C—Taking Action

Millie felt sick. Her stomach churned with the intensity of the Snake River. She knew she didn't want to go through another period of isolation and hysteria. That simply was not productive.

Millie's sister-in-law, Brenda, had been calling on her to get a "beauty make-over"—one of those all-day affairs of pampering and pedicuring, massaging, waxing, curling, and rouging. Millie decided to do it. She also took along the want ads from the newspaper. Her plan was to look for work as a chef's assistant. The men in her support group would be proud of her. She invited all of them over for a finicky supper of artichoke, tabouli, seviche, steak tartare, and shadberry foole. They were becoming friends, Millie and these gay men.

Over time, since her early years of reclusiveness and living solely for her father, her brother, and Charlie, Millie learned that friends made salt sweet and blackness bright. She buttoned her coat, preparing to leave the house. She had a busy day ahead.

* * * * *

Phyllis attended a PFLAG meeting and came home chattering like a parrot in heat. She had some strong observations about gays and lesbians, which she readily shared with

Mark — as if they would be new to him. "One out of every ten men and women is gay, and he or she is probably gay from birth," Phyllis said, "which means it probably wasn't my fault; it was his father's genes. Come to think of it, Dan's father liked to rearrange the furniture and hated baseball."

Mark restrained himself for the twentieth time that day. Losing his temper wouldn't help. Being with Phyllis sometimes evoked the urge to kill, upsetting his usually pacific nature. It was time for Mark to get back into therapy. He phoned his friend Tommy, a therapist, and asked for a recommendation. He was tired of feeling this way.

* * * * *

Beaming like carefree juniors preparing for a prom, Carmen, Yolanda, and Inez went on a "shopping spree." Carmen wanted to spend her $200 stipend for speaking at an AIDS conference sponsored by the American Association of Physicians for Human Rights. At the conference, she merely told her story. That was enough for the audience of doctors to embrace her message.

Carmen had been wanting to get Inez a new pair of hot pink high-top sneakers and pink and green anklets. Yolanda deserved a new sweater. Little Xavier would get baseball uniform pajamas; Carmen would get earrings that resembled chandeliers; and Mama, bless her, would get something too, though Carmen didn't yet know what it was.

Four months before, Carmen had brought little Xavier home from the hospital. True to her word, Carmen was more attentive to Inez and the baby. Yolanda had her old girlfriend back. And for the first time, Carmen refused a speaking engagement and attended a PTA meeting instead.

Carmen continued lecturing on AIDS. To her audiences, she was living proof that it was not a "gay disease." Sometimes she spoke for a modest fee; often she did it for the public good. But unlike her past speaking "gigs," these recent com-

mitments never supplanted family time. The apartment, which had often become a shrine of neglect if Yolanda and Inez did not attend to it, was now spotless. Finally, Carmen was able to keep her house clean and be an attentive mother.

* * * * *

Earlier in this book, we mentioned that caregivers adapt to their loved one's AIDS in two basic ways: changing their *response* to the condition and changing their *environment*.

So far in our journey toward acceptance, we've talked about the first area—changing our responses. When we take the time to learn about AIDS and work with our feelings, we're focused on ourselves. In short, we're working on the world inside us, the world of knowledge and emotion.

In the basic text of Alcoholics Anonymous, one doctor writes of his own recovery from alcoholism, describes his approach to his insides, his feelings:

> *And acceptance is the answer to all my problems today. When I am disturbed, it is because I find some person, place, thing, or situation—some fact of my life—unacceptable to me, and I can find no serenity until I accept that person, place, thing, or situation as being exactly the way it is supposed to be at this moment.* [1]

This idea applies with equal force to caregivers.

THE POWER OF TAKING ACTION

As we move toward acceptance, however, we also have another strategy to draw on. Beyond changing ourselves, we can "change the world" in some significant way. We can choose to alter our environment, the places, and the events that make up daily life. Joining a support group, moving to a new house or a new city, cutting back to part-time work—these are common examples.

This chapter lists a number of actions people have taken to increase their effectiveness as caregivers. Keep in mind, though, that our suggestions are just that—suggestions. This list is not a litany of obligations or a schedule of demands. Nor is it an exhaustive list. We offer these suggestions as tools for the journey toward acceptance. Caregivers can consider what applies to them. And we can move slowly in taking action, making the small steps first.

It's not necessary to flood ourselves with change. Often, it works best to consider only one goal at a time, state it clearly, and divide it into small tasks. For example, Yolanda decides that she's temporarily burned out in her role as Carmen's caregiver. In working through this, she feels the well-meaning advice offered by friends falls short of the mark: "Just wait it out." "Things will get better." "You think you're having a hard time—just think about Carmen!" Yolanda feels strongly that she needs more.

So Yolanda's goal is to get professional help. Stated in that way, however, her goal sounds broad, vague, and even intimidating. It would be easy to postpone any action. An alternative is to first make the goal specific and concrete. She can turn the goal of "finding professional help" into "finding a counselor who knows a lot about AIDS, chemical dependency, and the Latino community. Call that person and make an appointment for a first session."

Next, Yolanda can divide and conquer. By this we mean brainstorming a list of smaller goals, each leading to the larger goal of finding a counselor. For example:

- Scan the Yellow Pages for a list of counselors
- Ask friends for the names of counselors
- Get a copy of a newsletter for people with AIDS
- Ask her personal doctor to recommend a therapist
- Check out a book from the library on counseling

Taking any one of these actions could well lead Yolanda to a solid recommendation for a counselor and some understanding of what to expect out of the therapy process.

Note that these tasks all have one thing in common: they are highly "doable." In fact, each task is so small that Yolanda could do any one of them *today*. Working in a similar way, we can build the momentum for action—even the far-reaching changes that can transform our life.

It's been said that the hardest part of attaining any goal is taking the first step. We can do two things to make that step possible: First, state our goal in a concrete, specific way, seeing it clearly in our minds. Second, make the first step toward that goal a small one. Each action taken in this spirit can fuel our motivation to do much more—especially as we start to get results in Phase C.

SUGGESTIONS FOR ACTION

Spend Time Away from the Person with AIDS

Our first suggestion is to step back occasionally—to let go of the caregiving role. This can be as simple as spending short amounts of time away from the people for whom we care. As a first step, we can list the activities and events that are fun, renewing, or relaxing for us. These vary widely, according to the needs of each caregiver. For some, a solitary walk in the early morning is enough. Other caregivers may want something more extensive—a meditation retreat, a separate vacation, or professional respite care from a home nurse or friend.

In any case, the essential thing is to schedule the time and activity we need. We can mark it on a calendar. And we can treat it with the same urgency we'd assign to a project at work or an appointment with the doctor. It's that important.

As caregivers, we can let our roles evolve. We can find a balance. Caregiving also has a rhythm, a cycle of activity and rest. At times, we're intensely involved, even preoccupied with the people for whom we care. This is the cycle of activity. At other times, we must nourish ourselves by spending time alone or cultivating our own interests. This is the cycle of rest. Rest frees us from being consumed by caregiving.

This passage from the Book of Ecclesiastes in the *Bible* sums up this aspect of caregiving:

> *For everything there is a season, and a time for every matter*
> *under heaven:*
> *a time to be born, and a time to die;*
> *a time to plant, and a time to pluck up what is planted;*
> *a time to kill, and a time to heal;*
> *a time to weep, and a time to laugh;*
> *a time to mourn, and a time to dance;*
> *a time to cast away stones, and a time to gather stones*
> *together;*
> *a time to embrace, and a time to refrain from*
> *embracing . . .* [2]

Enlarge the Scope of Concerns

We can also do more than take occasional breaks from the caregiving role. In fact, we can take action that affirms a life purpose beyond caregiving and AIDS.

In Chapter Eight we compared intense negative feelings to a pot boiling over on the stove. We talked about two responses to this event: turning down the flame (acknowledging the feeling) and opening the lid to see what's in the pot (observing the feeling). In enlarging the scope of our concerns, we find a third response: emptying the contents of the pot and pouring them into a larger container. That action decreases the explosive pressure.

While Charlie was still alive, he entered the hospital when he developed chronic pain in his stomach. His doctors decided to run a number of tests, and Charlie's hospitalization became an extended stay. For both medical and logistical reasons, Millie could not stay at the hospital much. Given this situation, it was tempting for Millie to express her utter codependence on Charlie: "Now he's gone. I can't stay by his side, but I still think about him constantly." Her impulse was to stay at home, look through photo albums of Charlie, surround herself with his belongings, and think about calling him four times each day.

A more healing alternative would be for Millie to focus on what *she* needs at the moment. She could take the initiative, call a friend and make plans to go out for dinner. She could talk to Brenda about what Charlie and she are going through. At the same time, she could also make it a point to talk about things *other* than Charlie. Beyond these, she can work part-time, volunteer, or become more active at church. Any of these actions could shake Millie out of codependence and cast her out of the role of victim.

For some of us, life "beyond" our loved one with AIDS involves service to others. As people who respond to AIDS daily, we can do much for others who are affected in any way by the condition. We can raise funds for an AIDS organization. Or we can join a support group for caregivers, offering our expertise and life experience to other AIDS caregivers. At the same time, we can detach ourselves in a healthy way from the person we care for. With the larger perspective and renewed energy that result, we can embrace the caregiving role with more energy and compassion.

This is Millie's view. After Charlie died, she volunteered as a buddy for a woman who had AIDS. That experience led her to say, "During the day I can work with AIDS and not think of Charlie. It's really healing to do the work I do. I have both the insight into AIDS and the emotions of a caregiver. But one way to feel better is to relate to a stranger and her issues, rather than the person I loved. Working with someone else gives one perspective on my feelings about Charlie and our life together. That's something I've never had before."

Some caregivers may feel that volunteer work, while drawing them out of their own caregiving relationship, is more than they can handle. "I live with AIDS twenty-four hours each day," Yolanda says. "I don't want to go out looking for more." It's important to admit this feeling and respond to it. These caregivers may prefer to enter a support group that focuses on *their* needs as caregivers. Most AIDS organizations offer such groups. Twelve Step groups such as Al-Anon may also help some of us. Such groups can also widen our network of friends, reducing our sense of isolation.

The labels *caregiver* or *those who care for a person with AIDS* do not define us. We are partly defined by *whom and what we love*. Besides other people, these may include our work, a hobby, a volunteer project, a subject studied in school, or any other abiding interest. It's important to sustain and cultivate these interests, even in the face of AIDS. Having an illness, or caring for someone with the illness, need not divorce us from what we're enthusiastic about. We can expand our sense of self by enlarging our involvement with other people and interests.

Encourage the Person You Care For To Reach Out to Others

The previous suggestion spoke of the common need to offer the caregiver perspective. This point applies with equal force to the person with AIDS. The people we care for also cry out for a life purpose that transcends their partial identities as "persons with AIDS." We may not even hear this cry, something that reminds us to heed their unspoken needs.

People with AIDS often feel better when they counsel others with the same condition, do volunteer work for AIDS organizations, or talk to others about AIDS. Such action puts the "helper-therapy" principle to work: in activity that serves others, the "helper" is healed as much as the person being helped.

This is a central principle in the Twelve Steps. In fact, the Twelfth Step of Alcoholics Anonymous states it explicitly:

> *Having had a spiritual awakening as the result of these steps, we tried to carry this message to alcoholics, and to practice these principles in all our affairs.*[3]

And in the Twelve Steps for people with HIV illness, we find the same idea:

> *Having had a spiritual awakening as a result of these steps, we tried to carry this message to other HIV infected people, and to practice these principles in all our affairs.*[4]

The dynamic of reaching out is a cornerstone of recovery in the Twelve Step programs for addiction to alcohol or other drugs. Likewise, it can be an important component of problem solving and healing with AIDS.

Remember to See the Whole Person

The person with AIDS is first a person—not a "patient" or an "AIDS victim." In fact, the term *victim* is best discarded from our vocabulary. None of us need be a victim unless we choose to be.

Likewise, the person with AIDS is a patient only some of the time. And he or she is always more than a patient. We can describe AIDS in relation to the people we care for; yet in doing so, we have not fully described any of them. A human being, even with a chronic illness, is more than a bag of skin containing a bunch of symptoms. A person is more than a diagnosis. A person is not defined by illness any more than we are defined by our job titles, our height and weight, or our street address.

Ram Dass and Paul Gorman underscore this point in *How Can I Help?*—a wonderful book on caregiving. They quote the words of a woman who longs to be affirmed as a person beyond her symptoms:

> *I've been chronically ill for twelve years. Stroke. Paralysis. That's what I'm dealing with now. I've gone to rehab*

> program after rehab program. . . . But I must say this:
> I have never, ever, met someone who sees me as a
> whole. . . . [5]

This woman puts the issue in plain terms: She is more than
a problem to fix, a case to solve, or a patient who requires
care. Unless we remind ourselves of this as we care for people
with AIDS, we'll miss what's important. We'll risk merely
patching things over with Band-Aids.

Take Care of Your Own Health

Some caregivers are so completely "on call" for the person
with AIDS that they lose contact with their own bodies. This
was the case with Millie, who religiously monitored all of
Charlie's symptoms. She responded to his every cough,
treated each cut as life threatening, and dispensed medication at exactly the time ordered by the doctor. Yet, she
awakened one day to pain in her lower back, tight shoulders,
and a severe cold—conditions she had no idea were developing. In her obsession with Charlie's health, she ignored the
warning signals from her own body.

As caregivers, it helps to wake each morning and briefly review our own physical condition. We can ask some key
questions:

- "How is *my* energy level, anyway?"
- "Am I getting enough rest?"
- "What's my diet been like this past month?"

And as we respond to these questions, we can take the appropriate action.

As a further step, we can remind the person with AIDS that
caregivers need care too. We can ask our loved ones to recognize that all of us are going through similar emotions. Even
though the objects of those feelings may differ for the
caregiver and the person with AIDS, the dynamics of the feel-

ings may be largely the same. Though both Dan and Mark were afraid much of the time, Mark could ask Dan for a hug—and both felt better.

Spend Time with the Person You Care For— Without Focusing on AIDS

Even in our relationship to people with AIDS, we do not have to constantly deal with illness. We can read together, attend concerts, go shopping, and invite friends over. We can have fun without discussing AIDS. We can continue to make decisions. And we can keep making plans for the future.

This is the attitude of living with AIDS and moving beyond it. Such an attitude is basic to living well with any chronic illness, and it's most typical of Stage Three (coasting) behavior. As Dan said to Mark: "Let's go have fun and leave Auntie AIDS behind." This is another way of taking action based on the strategy of positive denial.

Overcome Isolation

Because we fear rejection from friends, family, and society, people with AIDS and their caregivers commonly report feeling like "two against the world." They feel cut off, rejected, ostracized.

Ironically, this special feature of coping with AIDS makes it all the more crucial for us to overcome our isolation. We can seek out family members and friends who *will* listen. In doing so, it's important to stay in contact with those who know about and understand our loved one's AIDS. Nevertheless, we can still find help from people who don't know but still care about us. In Chapter Eight we spoke of the advantages of positive denial—of not thinking about AIDS all the time. In a similar way, it's not necessary to tell everyone about AIDS. We can enjoy nurturing relationships at many levels.

Fortunately, attitudes toward AIDS are changing, even if

they are painfully slow. In most cities, AIDS organizations and support groups are established; many are growing steadily. In our efforts to overcome isolation, we can begin with them. These can be especially valuable when we find it hard to tell friends and family what we're going through. If need be, we can also seek professional help.

Getting professional help does not mean paying vast sums of money to a psychiatrist for endless sessions on the couch. Instead, we have wide-ranging options: counseling hot lines, employee assistance programs, free self-help groups, members of the clergy, therapists who offer short-term therapies or sliding fee scales, and peer counselors at local AIDS organizations.

In fact, our capacity to be effective caregivers is directly related to our ability to receive help, whether formal or informal. And as we reach out to others—especially to other caregivers—we rediscover a basic truth: We are not alone. Thousands of others are coping with the discovery of AIDS, adapting to that fact, coasting, and facing collisions. Like us, they are finding their way through each stage in the caregiving journey. And like us, they are moving through those stages without clear answers. Though we can offer few certainties about AIDS, we can share our perspectives. We can hold hands, cry together, laugh together, and comfort each other. We can simply *be* together, and many times that will be enough.

Talk to the Person with AIDS About Whom to Tell

As we saw in Part Two of this book, caregivers face a difficult question early in their journey: "Will I tell other people that the person I love has AIDS? And what will I do if the person with AIDS doesn't want anyone to know?"

All of the people in our vignettes grapple with this issue. Part of their impulse to keep AIDS a secret is a realistic fear of discrimination—loss of jobs, homes, insurance, and other benefits. The other reason for not telling is often based on shame, guilt, or embarrassment—the desire to hide.

We must balance this desire against our need for emotional health. To be healthy, we must tell someone about what we're experiencing as caregivers. And sharing our stories becomes a given if we enter therapy, join a support group, or participate in a Twelve Step program.

In this book, we cannot offer specific advice to any person with AIDS or to a caregiver. In each case, people must decide for themselves who will know and who won't. Even so, we can offer two principles that promote healthy relationships and healthy disclosure.

One is to tell, but tell selectively. We can rightly be choosey about who should know. Mark and Dan, for example, tell their close friends about AIDS long before Dan's ready to tell his mother. He feels strongly that support and understanding will come more readily from them than from his family. In contrast, Carmen tells everyone about her AIDS, and she's forced to live with the consequences: rejection from neighbors and loss of her apartment. Millie, despite Charlie's admonition, chooses a trusted family member, Brenda, to tell. Each demonstrate the process of selective disclosure. If we hold information from some, we must face the consequences when they do find out.

A second principle is to keep this issue in the open with the people we care for. In this book, we don't offer specific guidelines about whom to tell. We can, however, underline a general principle: Things work best when the decision about whom to tell is a joint decision—one on which the person with AIDS and the caregiver both agree.

Turn to Healing Practices

Affirmation, visualizations, meditation, relaxation—each of these techniques can free up our energy and cast out negative emotions. As such, they can empower us as caregivers. In some form, they can become part of our daily routine.

In most cases, these techniques are based on simple ideas. For example, the principle behind affirmations is to replace negative messages with positive ones. Take the thoughts that some caregivers hold just below their conscious awareness: *I'm not capable enough to take care of someone who's really sick. . . . I'm not really doing anything to help. . . . No one really cares about what I'm feeling, anyway. . . .* Through sheer repetition, such ideas can frustrate every action we take by becoming our reality.

These ideas are messages to our subconscious. To counter them, we can meet them in the same level of the mind. Replacing them with positive statements that appeal to the subconscious makes a lot of sense.

Effective affirmations have several things in common. For one, they are simple and direct statements—single, short sentences work best. Such statements are detailed and specific. They are written in present tense and stated in positive rather than negative terms. In addition, they describe a desired condition as if it has *already been attained.* Examples of affirmations for caregivers are:

- *I am a capable and compassionate caregiver.*
- *In any situation, I trust myself to make the most healing response.*
- *I am knowledgeable about AIDS.*
- *When negative feelings arise in me, I let them go instantly.*

Affirmations can be even more effective when paired with visualizations. In Chapter Eight we spoke of the role of negative mental pictures in creating negative emotions. Using the same dynamic, we create positive emotions by changing the nature of those pictures.

The essence of working with your imagination is picturing *in detail* what you want. For example, visualization tapes are available to help people with AIDS envision a healthy immune system, see their bodies regaining strength, and "hear" their bodies telling them about the best course of treatment.

This technique is finding its way into mainstream medicine as well. Carl Simonton, M.D., pioneered the use of visualization with cancer patients. His patients had a survival rate twice that of the national norm.

Two advocates for visualization and affirmation are George Melton and the late Wil Garcia. In 1985, both of them were diagnosed with HIV illness — Melton with ARC, and Garcia with AIDS. After trying a number of therapies with little effect, they found inspiration in the ideas of Simonton, Louise Hay, Bernie Siegel, M.D., and others who emphasize the role of the mind and emotions in healing disease.

Writing in *Beyond AIDS: A Journey Into Healing,* Melton talks about the unique character of Garcia's visualizations:

> *Instead of continuing to attack and kill the virus, he began to visualize an energy of love coming into his body through the top of his head. This energy spread slowly throughout his body and down into his legs where his lesions were. Gently he began to stroke the lesions with this energy, caressing them softly. He visualized this love energy totally enveloping the virus. He then began talking to it softly. He reassured it that it was in a safe and loving body. It was so safe, in fact, it could feel free to go to sleep if it wanted to.* [6]

Visualization and affirmations can be combined with other techniques such as meditation and progressive relaxation. As such, visualization and affirmations can be even more powerful. Explaining any of these techniques in more detail is beyond the scope of this book. Many other materials do offer specific help. Some of them are listed in Appendix Four, under Recommended Materials on AIDS and Caregiving.

Join a Twelve Step Program

For recovering people or others involved in a Twelve Step group, it's essential to keep the program alive. That means "working the program"—living out the ideas and actions described in each Step. This applies to Mark, Carmen, and Yolanda, all of whom are working to recover from chemical dependency. In each case, staying grounded in recovery can help them live better with AIDS and increase their skill as caregivers as well as human beings.

Yet we need not be chemically dependent to benefit from a Twelve Step group. Other groups adapt the Twelve Step philosophy to a variety of goals—for example, overcoming codependence, food addiction, negative emotions, and many more. Millie, for example, attends Al-Anon, a program for members of an alcoholic's family. Likewise, some of us may benefit from Emotions Anonymous, Overeaters Anonymous, Gamblers Anonymous, or similar groups grounded in the Twelve Step tradition. Special Alcoholics Anonymous groups exist for people with AIDS and those concerned about HIV infection (HIVIES, Alcoholics Anonymous for AIDS Awareness, and others).

Keep a Journal

Much of what people gain in any counseling or psychotherapy is perspective, detachment, and greater awareness. We can promote each of these goals by writing. In writing, we can narrate our experience and let clarity and coherence emerge from the tumult of daily life. This has real healing potential.

Many people have also discovered that journals are a powerful way to formulate and preserve the lessons from our caregiving experience.

Work Creatively with Burnout

As caregivers, we deal constantly with our reactions to the thoughts, feelings, and behavior of those we care for. Sooner or later, however, many caregivers deal with an overall response to the whole experience of caregiving. Most commonly it's called *burnout*.

That we might experience burnout is not surprising. The chronic illness, social stigma, and uncertainties of AIDS raise as many issues as any sane person would care to deal with in one lifetime. It's natural to feel overwhelmed by all this and want to be released from the caregiving role.

The trick is to cope with burnout before it poisons our relationship with the people we care for. Toward this end, we can keep two things in mind: (1) working skillfully with our feelings, and (2) avoiding codependence.

In Chapter Eight we talked at length about Phase B: how to work with feelings. We applied our ideas to negative feelings such as fear, sadness, and anxiety. Everything we said there applies to burnout. Like any other feeling, burnout arises in us as thoughts and sensations in the body. To work effectively with such feelings, we can name them, accept them, and observe them precisely. Doing so helps us shift into the position of observing our feelings with calmness and detachment. In turn, that loosens the grip of the emotion. With this perspective, we can defuse burnout before it becomes a collision in Stage Four.

To avoid burnout, we can also remind ourselves of the dangers of codependence. For caregivers, what does this mean? In essence, letting go of the impulse to control, to fix, to perfect, and to heal the people we love.

Instead of trying to control the people we love, we can focus our attention, discard our private agendas, and really listen. In doing so, we can truly help the people we love. We often find that much helping is still getting done—even though we feel like we're "doing nothing."

Much of our effectiveness as caregivers consists in one thing: *our ability to live with the fact that there may be no neat or absolute "solution" for AIDS or for our life.* We cannot cure disease. Nor can we free those people we love from negative emotions or physical pain. And we may cycle through the stages of discovery, adapting, coasting, and overcoming collisions again and again. Still, we can be there for each other. In *How Can I Help?* Ram Dass and Paul Gorman express it this way:

> *But perhaps there will be nothing we can* do. *Then we can only* be, *and* be with *the person in his or her pain, attending to the quality of our* own *consciousness. On his or her behalf, we will dwell in whatever truth and understanding we have come to which is beyond suffering. From this, compassion arises. Hearts that have known pain meet in mutual recognition and trust.*[7]

This passage speaks of something that is "beyond suffering." We who care for someone with AIDS may balk at the idea that anything is beyond suffering. Some of us feel our own suffering in each day, hour, or minute. Yet, while it's not possible to erase pain or discomfort from our life, we can lessen the sense of suffering they bring. Doing so calls on us to move to a new phase: acceptance.

CHAPTER 10

Phase D—Acceptance

Charlie was gone. Charlene and Millie had come to an understanding about Odell and his limitations. And Millie was done trying to change her daughter's mind about him. She let go. She gave up. And so the rift between mother and daughter healed.

Millie showered love on her grandchildren. She attended church, and she was amused as she contrasted the memories of her Baptist upbringing with the folksinging and informality of the Metropolitan Community Church. This was the church to which her gay friends belonged. For the first time in years she felt in the presence of God. She felt at home.

* * * * *

Dan was home from the hospital, finally. It was a relief for the three of them. Dan seemed a little weaker and a little mellower—calmer and more at peace than Mark had ever seen him, especially around Phyllis.

Dan's newfound calm appealed to Phyllis and Mark, and it seemed to rub off on them. Dinner that evening was pleasant. Conversation was easy, with genuine sharing. It was as if they realized how important they were to one another.

* * * * *

"Open your eyes and go in peace," said the channeler, a disciple of Louise Hay. Carmen arose and found her way to

the door, stopping to greet other group members and say good-bye. She'd come to depend on the weekly meditation and visualization sessions, and she was glad she'd finally gotten Inez into a support group of her own.

Little Xavier was still well, and Inez's headaches had subsided; Carmen was grateful. As she left the building, she met Inez and Yolanda, flushed with excitement about the movie they'd just seen. Arm in arm, they all headed out for ice cream.

* * * * *

By the time our loved one has lived with AIDS for a while, we know full well about the superficial, if well-meant, comforts other people offer us. "Suffering is God's way of bringing people together," says Hermenia, Carmen's mother. Yolanda, trying to offer comfort, says much the same thing: "Facing death makes human life all the more precious. Knowing that our days may be shortened helps us live better today."

Depending on our emotional state at the time we hear such words, they may truly reassure us. Or, they may sear through us to that core of pain inside. For Mark, they affirm an unspoken conviction: *No one really understands what I go through each day caring for Dan. When I talk about AIDS or what's happening in our lives, people get uncomfortable. They avert their eyes, change the subject, or leave the conversation. They just don't want to deal with it. I really am alone.*

FACING SUFFERING, FACING OURSELVES

Here we face more than the stigma surrounding AIDS. We confront directly a deeper and more pervasive matter: the taboo against talking about suffering, limitation, and death. The mere mention of AIDS brings images of mortality and pain to the minds of most people: young men in hospital wards, connected to respirators and IV tubes, with sallow skin and glazed eyes. People waiting to die. We know that people can live well with HIV illness, carry on their lives, work productively, love, and experience health. But to many people, this seems like an impossible contradiction. For some of them, the contradiction is so great that they turn away from AIDS entirely.

Despite what we caregivers learn about AIDS, the popular, negative images may still seize us. When we feel the grip of panic, despair, shock, or sadness, our mind and heart may close. We may even imagine and assume the worst. We, too, may want to turn away and run.

AIDS has the power to shatter society's denial of death. We, too, may grow sick and suffer. We, too, may die. Many prefer not to hear this reminder, a human tendency that's been around for thousands of years. The *Mahabharata*, an ancient poem from the Hindu tradition, offers one example. In this tale, a spirit poses a riddle to a young man, Yudishthira. If Yudishthira can answer the riddle correctly, his life will be saved; if he fails, he will die. The riddle is: "What is the greatest wonder of all?" In his wisdom, Yudishthira replies correctly. "Every day, all around us, Death takes lives beyond counting, yet those who live think, Death can never come this day to me."

In the face of all this we can well ask, "Is the person with AIDS really that much different from us?"

- We have the potential to love, work, and learn; so does the person with AIDS.
- We can affirm life or shrink from it; so can the person with AIDS.
- We can face the fact of death squarely and come to terms with it; so can the person with AIDS.

Such issues are raised with special intensity for a person with AIDS; this person faces the possibility of death sooner than others. But as caregivers, these are our questions as well. They are the questions for every human being, in every time and place. The person with AIDS is a mirror for all of us. In the faces, hearts, and minds of the people we care for, we see ourselves.

As caregivers, we're reminded of a central fact: The way we relate to another's suffering is intimately tied to the way we relate to our own suffering. In *How Can I Help?*, Ram Dass and Paul Gorman write of this:

> *Part of it is dealing with our own aversion to suffering in and of itself. There is, for example, the early warning system of denial which often comes into play almost automatically. We blot out the suffering right before our eyes. We walk down the street past beggars and people obviously in pain without even noticing them. An ambulance goes by; it's just a loud noise, it'll pass. We hear cries in the night; it's only a family feud, we turn over and go back to sleep. Potential nuclear annihilation is only twenty minutes away; we can't handle the thought of it. It's as if we have an invisible screen that deflects evidence of pain as soon as it gets close enough. How easily we delete it from awareness, without even being aware that we've done so.* [1]

And when we fear the presence of suffering in the people we care for, that fear grows and may feel overwhelming. This can lead to desperate attempts to erase the suffering. Ram Dass and Gorman call this the "we gotta syndrome":

> *Often what's happening is that 'we gotta' get rid of someone's pain because it's hurting us too much. This reactive urgency actually increases the suffering. It's Typhoid Mary disguised as Florence Nightingale.* [2]

THE POTENTIAL FOR AWAKENING

Even so, caring for someone with AIDS can bring forth a new potential in us; in fact, it can *wake us up*. Because now we are confronted with the basic currents in human life: suffering, pain, and mortality; fear, uncertainty, and longing; hope, renewal, and transformation. The essential questions about the essence of our lives are thrown into sharp relief.

At times, so many of the issues that had occupied our days before life with AIDS seem distant, unimportant: making money, winning the political battles at work, accumulating more possessions, gaining professional status. Confronting a life-threatening disease has put us in touch with something more fundamental and important.

It's possible for this realization to lift us to a higher state of attention. When we see our loved one in pain, we can be riveted to the present. Our mind can be focused, alert, and concentrated. Our loved one's suffering can become heaven and earth for us in that moment. The mind may cease its flow of random images and thoughts. For a moment, it may become as still as a placid lake or as turbulent as the rapids before a waterfall.

Any of the great spiritual traditions teach that moments are infinitely precious. With the moments of stillness may come clarity, concentration, energy, and profound teachings. In *The Color of Light: Meditations for All of Us Living with AIDS*, Perry Tilleraas writes:

> *When we see other people suffering, it's hard to accept it, just as it's difficult to view AIDS as anything but a tragedy. But AIDS is a teacher for all of us. We're learning things such as how to accept love, how to give unconditional love, how to trust, how to die, how to live, how to stand up and be empowered, how to let go, how to surrender, and how to ask for help.* [3]

Can we as caregivers open ourselves to the teachings of AIDS? Much of that depends on our capacity to remain open in two ways: (1) finding our own spirituality and (2) discovering our own source of serenity. With these two areas, we caregivers can take two giant steps on our journey toward acceptance.

Twelve Step groups such as Alcoholics Anonymous offer help for that journey. Those who join AA find it's essential to keep one thing in mind: Twelve Step ideas don't call for belief or unquestioning acceptance. Applying the Steps does not mean blindly accepting the teachings of any group. In fact, Twelve Step concepts may deepen the philosophic or religious perspectives we already have.

We're not dealing with religious creed or dogma here. There is no need for religious conversion of any kind. Instead, the Twelve Step tradition centers on *practices* and *perspectives*. Examples of common practices are prayer and meditation. These we can define in individual ways; we can use them in ways that are personally meaningful. And instead of adhering to rigid definitions of God or Higher Power, we can merely assume that help is available to us from many sources —if only we are open to them.

This, in essence, is faith. One person quoted in the basic text of Alcoholics Anonymous states it this way: *"It was only a matter of being willing to believe in a Power greater than myself. Nothing more was required of me to make my beginning."*[4] With that perspective, we open ourselves to spirituality.

OUR QUEST FOR SPIRITUALITY

The Twelve Steps speak openly of spiritual matters. We can quote some of those Steps in particular:

2. Came to believe that a Power greater than ourselves could restore us to sanity.
3. Made a decision to turn our will and our lives over to the care of God *as we understood Him.*
11. Sought through prayer and meditation to improve our conscious contact with God *as we understood Him,* pray-

ing only for knowledge of His will for us and the power to carry that out.

12. Having had a spiritual awakening as the result of these steps, we tried to carry this message to alcoholics, and to practice these principles in all our affairs.[5]

How Religion and Spirituality Differ

On reading these Steps for the first time, many of us may share Mark's first reaction: "Accepting the Twelve Steps means buying into a lot of religious baloney. I'm not a church person, and that language just turns me off."

This reaction makes less sense when we understand the difference between *spirituality* and *religion.* Many religions have to do with dogma, creeds, belief systems, and formal ceremonies. Spirituality, on the other hand, need not have anything to do with these. This is true for several reasons.

First is the use of the term *God.* The Twelve Steps are explicit in speaking of God *as we understand God.* And that qualification is crucial. No single definition of God is offered or imposed on anyone by the Twelve Steps. This is an idea for each of us to define individually. In many cases, the Twelve Step programs use the more neutral term, Higher Power. Many people prefer this term over the emotionally laden term, God.

God, Higher Power—both of these terms refer to something other than the tenets established by any formal religious group. Ultimately, they refer to a source of help in our life—any source of help outside of ourselves and greater than ourselves. Before alcoholics enter treatment, most share a common characteristic: They refuse to accept help. In fact, they may hotly deny that they have a problem or need any help. Their delusion is that they can stop drinking at any time, simply as an act of will. At that point, they are beyond and above help.

When an alcoholic takes Step One to heart—"We admitted

we were powerless over alcohol—that our lives had become unmanageable,"—he or she brings the possibility of healing into his or her life. By admitting powerlessness over drinking, we become open to help. This is the same as opening ourselves to a Higher Power.

With the Twelve Steps, people may begin by thinking of any source of help as their Higher Power. In fact, an alcoholic's Higher Power may be anything that finally brings him or her to treatment: a passage from a book; the intervention of a spouse, friend, or employer; the pain of a child. Others may define their Higher Power as the life force, the universe, a loving parent, nature, or the Twelve Step group itself. Any of these can be a source of energy, strength, and comfort to people. Any of them can act as God or Higher Power.

In short, the *content* of our definition of Higher Power does not matter. What is essential is how we use this force in our life—how we act, what we do today. It only matters that we open ourselves to a source of help—whatever that source may be. What's more, we can turn to that source when we freely admit our powerlessness to fix, manipulate, or control other people or events in our life. This is an empowering message for us as caregivers.

Admitting Powerlessness

The fact is that we are powerless over many aspects of AIDS in the people we love. We cannot command the virus out of their bodies or deliver a cure. We cannot rid them of disease or even make them choose healthy behaviors. We cannot control their actions, feelings, and thoughts in response to AIDS. In short, we cannot *make* them do anything.

As caregivers, our powerlessness over AIDS is driven home constantly. The person we love may be fine today. If we've moved from Stage Two into Stage Three, it may even be possible to forget about the illness. At times, nothing seems wrong. Our loved one looks and feels fine. All symptoms may be gone for the moment. We can work, laugh, play, and talk just like we used to.

And yet, a common cold may be the first step toward a long hospital stay. Tumors or lesions can develop, seemingly out of nowhere. A miracle drug taken with hopes of remission can produce side-effects that make matters worse. In short, the health of the person we love is precarious. That means one thing for us as caregivers: Our lives can change dramatically in a single year, a single day, a single hour. Now, nothing is forever.

Given this fact, it's tempting to do everything we can to make things right again. And the most obvious thing to do is try and "fix" the external circumstances of our life. Too often that means grasping at anything offering the dimmest hope of reducing symptoms or arresting the illness. It can mean trying every experimental therapy or shopping for the right specialist.

Such grasping can also mean trying to take control of the other's life. And that can lead to a blurring of identities— feeling that we are responsible for our loved one's pain. This is the case with Inez. She reasons this way: "Mama really depends on me. Grandma, Yolanda, and I are everything she's got. I've got to stay out of trouble. I don't dare rock the boat or mess up, or things will just get worse for Mama. She'll just get sick. It's up to me to make sure she doesn't get sick again."

This quest for control can surface in a hundred ways, as it does for the people in our vignettes. Millie nagged at Charlie to test for HIV again and again. She harped at him to take medication. She insisted that he go to bed earlier and closely monitored the clock. Every morning she reminded Charlie to call for a doctor's appointment. Eventually, she made the appointment herself and let Charlie know only *after* the fact. She took over, desperately trying to control the uncontrollable: AIDS. Still, Charlie died. And there was nothing she could do for him in the end but bury and remember him.

When it comes to AIDS, we cannot fix the person we love.

We cannot guarantee that person long life and health. We must realize as caregivers we are *not God*. It is not in our power to dispense health and cure disease for the person we love. We cannot raise the dead, make the blind see or the crippled walk, or perform any other miracle of biblical proportions. And yet, the codependent caregiver is, in many ways, hoping to do just that.

The truth is: someone we love has AIDS; we do not. The people we care for have one path to walk; as caregivers, we have a different one. We can walk by the side of the person with AIDS; we can stay near him or her, but we cannot make the journey in that person's place.

Much of this has to do with understanding our limits as caregivers. Claudia Black stresses setting limits, for example, in overcoming false guilt and shame. We can work to establish healthy limits for ourselves:

> *"Dan is sick, and I don't know why," says Mark. "If I had something to do with this, it was accidental. I couldn't have known any better at the time. If I acted unwisely, I'm sorry for what I did. But I can't help him by blaming myself."*

> *"I did the best for Carmen that I could," says her mother. "I wish she had more advantages growing up, but she didn't. I wish her father wasn't such a louse, but he was. I wish there was something I could have done to help her avoid the drugs and this horrible virus. But there wasn't."*

Gratitude and Forgiveness

Some elements of spirituality are so down-to-earth that it's easy to forget them. One is gratitude, the ability to put aside for a moment all the things we feel are lacking and to focus on what we have. Each person can make a gratitude list that is an individual matter and will be different from any others. Most of us, though, can be thankful for having basic needs satisfied: health, having enough to eat, having a roof over our heads, and an income that satisfies many of our needs.

Our list can include people: friends who are still in contact, concerned family members, and people in support groups. Along with them we can list the things that give us pleasure, including our abilities, interests, hobbies, and skills. With a minimum of imagination, we can expand our gratitude list indefinitely. And simply by going through this exercise, we can feel a subtle healing taking place.

Along with gratitude for what we've been given comes the ability to forgive. Harboring resentments, stockpiling anger, making long mental lists of how we've been wronged — each of these robs us of energy. Such attitudes create emotional baggage that weigh us down.

There is an alternative. We can let go of bitterness, using the ideas for working with feelings described in Chapter Eight. We can forget others' shortcomings — and our own. In doing so, we actually feel lighter.

Millie can forgive Charlie for his secrets and his emotional coldness. "It doesn't mean I condone what he did," she points out. "Rather, forgiveness allows me to admit that Charlie did everything he could at the time. I can remember the pain he was in, all the things he was going through in facing up to AIDS."

Likewise, Yolanda can forgive Xavier for failing to be the perfect mate for Carmen. "If I keep on hating him," Yolanda points out, "he's still got a kind of power over me. Then he's still on my mind, taking up my time, making me feel bad. I can admit that he was once part of our lives. But now he's gone. Today is different, and I can always remember that."

In Surrendering, We Win

When we admit our powerlessness, in keeping with the wisdom of Step One, and when we open ourselves to sources of help, no matter where they appear in our life, we encounter a paradox: In surrendering, we win. In acknowledging error, we see the truth. In admitting powerlessness, we are empowered. By acknowledging helplessness, we are helped. We cannot resolve this paradox at the level of our mind. We can, however, realize this truth in the way we act, the way we live out our life. Doing this is really the core of Twelve Step programs.

After all, our task as caregivers is not to cure the person with AIDS, but to *let the healing in.* What it takes to heal is already present in the situation, in the person we love; it only needs to be unleashed, unblocked. Techniques that involve drugs, surgery, medication, affirmations, visualizations, and other sources do not actually cure people or wipe out their disease. Instead, they merely reinforce the body's own ability to heal itself. That ability is a healing, transforming force present in living things. Though that force has been called by many names—*Higher Power, God,* and others—we need not name it. We need only learn to cooperate with it.

How do we begin opening ourselves to help? By asking these questions:

- "What are the sources of strength in my life? What activities, people, or influences give me hope?"
- "When I get depressed, sad, or angry, what is it that restores a positive attitude?"
- "What are my passions and my interests? What are the things I really care about? Who are the people I really care for?"
- "What is it that wakes me up from everyday routine and allows me to feel intensely alive?"
- "What in my life helps me see things clearly? What experiences help me put things in true perspective? When am I in touch with what I truly value and wish to preserve? What is most important to me?"

Our answers to such questions will slowly reveal our Higher Power. Spirituality simply means opening up to our personal sources of strength and hope. For this is the essential nature of any Higher Power: It *acts* within us. It changes, soothes, heals, renews, and sustains us. *God* or *Higher Power* is only a name we assign to something that *happens* inside us. As the late Buckminister Fuller observed, "God is not a noun but a verb."

To live in this way is to live the spiritual life spoken of in the Twelve Steps. For some people, this may mean attending a church, taking part in religious ceremonies, and finding new meaning in traditional creeds. To others, though, spirituality may not surface in these ways. Often the simple practices that we pursue in the midst of daily life may be the richest source of spirituality.

Prayer and Meditation

The Twelve Steps speak in particular of two such practices: prayer and meditation. Again, some of us may initially balk at these terms. Just as with Higher Power or God, however, the Steps impose no rigid definition of prayer or meditation. Again, we are free to practice these in our own way.

Meditation, for example, can simply mean being quiet and fully present in the moment, without belief or expectation. And we can think of prayer as being the central wish in our life, our deepest desire—what we truly ask of life. In doing so, it helps to apply what Mark found: "Praying for God's will and not mine brings me relief. It reminds me that I'm not responsible for every outcome, that the universe doesn't center on me. I can let go of things and turn them over to my Higher Power and trust that whatever happens is supposed to happen."

Prayer and meditation, then, are simply remaining open to the healing, transforming force in our life. As such, they can take many different forms, and each of us can find our own methods. What matters most is that we stay in "conscious contact" with our sources of strength—whatever they may be.

Elene Loecher, a chemical dependency counselor, offers five suggestions for meditating. These are not rules or formulas. Rather, we can take them only as possible ways to open up spiritually:

1. *Establish a regular time for meditation.* This time will differ for each of us. Some people like early morning or late evening. For others, a time set aside in the middle of the day works best.

2. *Find a regular place and posture for meditating.* What we do while meditating varies widely. Some find solace in nature—slowly walking in the woods or sitting quietly by a stream. But our preferred place could also be a special room at home or work. The goal is finding a setting where we feel free from everyday concerns, relaxed, and alert.

3. *Focus attention on the chosen task.* The crux of meditation is to relax the body, calm the mind, and focus attention on a single object. Music or meditation tapes and books may help us accomplish these goals. If we meditate outdoors, the sounds of nature may give us useful objects: the rush of an ocean or lake, calls of birds, or wind rustling trees. Others may choose a physical object as the seed for meditation: a candle, seashell, flower, painting, or sculpture. Along with these, some of us may choose simple stretches or Yoga postures to help calm the mind.

4. *Allow our Higher Power to work.* If we're reading a book, notes Loecher, we can "pay attention to what jumps off the page. Chew on it—allow it to happen inside you without controlling it." In any case, she advises, "listen for the *invitations* in your life." Invitations are simply thoughts, images, or experiences that can bring us insight. In the spacious, calm atmosphere provided by meditation, we can hear these insights more clearly.

This, in effect, is allowing our Higher Power to "speak."

Such invitations may arise as we remember moments of sadness or joy. They may come from recalling a poignant memory, remembering an especially moving scene from a movie or play, or looking at a photograph that brings tears to our eyes. Some people find visual images offer invitations. For example, we might envision placing our resentments in a backpack, hiking to a mountain top, and asking that the pack be emptied for the return trip.

Writing can be especially powerful during meditation. We might write a dialogue with a person we love or at whom we feel angry. We can write messages to our Higher Power, thereby getting a handle on that for which we truly wish. Or we can simply record thoughts and feelings as they occur to us in a daily journal. In any case, it helps to write quickly, without pausing to change or edit words. Writing in this way, we may make many discoveries about ourselves and others.

5. *Gently close the meditation.* Making a smooth transition back to everyday life is an important part of meditation. We may choose to sit quietly for a minute or two before resuming normal activity. We may repeat an affirmation or memorized passage from a book. Or, we might say a simple prayer that's not tied to any formal religious belief. Many people choose the traditional Serenity Prayer:

> *God grant me the serenity*
> *To accept the things I cannot change,*
> *The courage to change the things I can,*
> *And the wisdom to know the difference.*

In the end, meditation and prayer are simply ways to attain the goals of the spiritual life. Among them are patience, sta-

bility, and a willingness to forgive others. These are the qualities referred to in the famous "love" passage from 1 Corin-
thians in the *Bible:*

> *Love is patient, love is kind, and is not jealous; love does
> not brag, and is not arrogant, does not act unbecomingly.
> It does not seek its own, is not provoked, does not take into
> account a wrong suffered, does not rejoice in unrighteous-
> ness, but rejoices with the truth, bears all things, believes
> all things, hopes all things, endures all things. Love never
> fails.*[6]

These ideas can deepen the quality and pleasure in our life.
And they can return us to caregiving with more energy and
compassion. In contrast, codependence drains us. It robs us
of energy and makes caregiving a burden. When we're
codependent, we wonder how we'll ever endure the next
day, the next hour, the next minute. By discovering spirituality, we open ourselves to sources that can truly help us bear
all things—including AIDS.

THE MEANING OF SERENITY

The mention of the Serenity Prayer returns us to another
question: What is serenity, anyway? As caregivers for people
with AIDS, can we really hope to find serenity? The answer
comes as we realize the nature of serenity. This word does
not refer to controlling the events in our lives. Instead, it
refers to how we *respond* to those events.

As much as any other act, caregiving brings this message
home. And a chronic illness such as AIDS reinforces the les-
son. As caregivers, we cannot determine the course of any infection or the success of any treatment for the people we love.
Ultimately, these are beyond our power. Yet we can choose
our responses to what life brings us. This is the whole art of
caregiving—and the art of being human.

During World War II, psychiatrist Viktor Frankl spent three

years at Auschwitz and other Nazi prison camps. In that time he lost most of his family and witnessed death nearly every day. Yet he made a discovery: even such circumstances cannot force some people to give up on life. Some prisoners knew that their loved ones still needed them; others felt strongly that they had valuable work to complete when they gained their freedom. By discovering meaning in such ways, many were able to survive the camps, both physically and emotionally. When speaking of the experience, Frankl quotes the philosopher Friedrich Nietzsche: "He who finds a *why* can bear almost any *how.*"

This led Frankl to believe that we have the ability to rise above any event. In *Man's Search for Meaning,* he wrote:

> *We who lived in concentration camps can remember the men who walked through the huts comforting others, giving away their last piece of bread. They may have been few in number, but they offer sufficient proof that everything can be taken from man but one thing: the last of human freedoms — to choose one's attitude in any given set of circumstances, to choose one's own way.*[7]

All of the tools for learning, working with feelings, and taking action offered in this book have a single goal: helping us find this freedom. This will not be easy. Reaching our goals will take time, patience, trials, and errors. We may often fail. We may still experience emotional or physical pain. At times we may forget what we've learned, sink into despair or depression, or forget to act on what we know.

Even so, we can forgive ourselves, just as we would forgive the people for whom we care. We can seek help from others. We can return to the sources of hope and strength in our life, and we can keep in contact with them. What's more, we can be grateful. We can treasure the moments of joy, laughter, ease, and contentment with the people we love, knowing that these are ours forever.

To speak of serenity in the face of AIDS is not enough.

Some people even move from accepting AIDS to embracing it. This recalls what Yolanda says about her treatment for addiction: "I really didn't start living until I got clean and sober. Before that, life was hell. But recovery has turned my life around and brought me so many gifts. Sometimes I can even say I'm glad I am an addict."

And of his own AIDS, George Melton writes:

> *Disease is a message from consciousness, spoken by the body. It needs to be faced with love, not suppressed out of fear. When we love ourselves totally because we know who we are, we love and accept our body's message. We then embrace its lesson.*[8]

In this spirit, we can truly speak of serenity as the peace that passes understanding. And it is this attitude of acceptance that we can slowly approach at each stage and phase of our journey as caregivers.

PART FOUR

TOMORROW

Epilogue

Millie was stuffing grape leaves, preparing for her dinner party the next night. She was working with her new partner, Murray, whom she'd met in the AIDS survivors' support group. They were laughing because in addition to three other gay men from the group, they were expecting Charlene, Odell, and Brenda.

Millie and Murray had opened a small catering business together. She'd cook; he'd be the front and finance person. And in the four months they'd been in business, Lox of Luck Catering had really taken off.

"My son-in-law is an excellent provider, and he loves my daughter," said Millie, "but he's really unsophisticated— even by my standards." They both laughed.

"If I come in a picture hat and sing Mame, will Odell think I'm singing about Vietnam?" asked Murray.

Millie laughed again. It felt good to be able to laugh again, and she really enjoyed Murray's camp sensibility. She wanted to share her new friends with her family.

* * * * *

It was one of the rare rainy nights in Phoenix—perfect for self-pity, old records, and facials. Phyllis had already gone to sleep, and Dan and Mark sat in bed. This was Dan's first day home from the hospital. The comfort of his own bed and familiar surroundings gave him pleasure.

"How much longer does your mother plan on staying?" asks Mark.

"She'll probably stay until the end of the week, to make sure I'm eating six meals a day," replies Dan.

"Are you still angry at me for telling her about you and us?" asks Mark.

"I was at first, but now that's passed. How can I stay angry at a man whom I consider one of the seven modern miracles?" smiles Dan.

That's one of the things Mark loved about Dan: his willingness to accept things and forgive. The men spent the rest of the evening talking about trips to places far away and exotic. They talked about splitting Dan's ashes — half for Mark (the bottom half) and half for Phyllis for the family plot. And they talked about loving each other forever.

* * * * *

Carmen, Yolanda, and Inez were coming home from the baby's wake. They had just dropped off Hermenia. Following right behind was Xavier, who was trying to get into the apartment building past Yolanda. A formidable obstacle, she was standing in the doorway, insisting that he was not welcome. Carmen cried and said she still loved him, but she knew things would not work out for them. And Xavier understood. He was an impediment to her sobriety, truly a bad influence on her.

Yolanda stood on the stoop waiting until Xavier was out of view. When she walked into the small apartment, Carmen was cradling and rocking Inez in her lap, back and forth. The place seemed empty without little Xavier.

Carmen was attempting to comfort Inez, who was crying because she feared Carmen would die too. "I don't want you to leave me, Mama," she sobbed. Carmen kept rocking the girl in her arms, assuring her that "Mama's going to be around awhile. We're all going to be fine, and we're all going to be together. You, Yolanda, Grandma, and me." Yolanda bent down to embrace them both, and she prayed to God that that would be so.

* * * * *

The final messages of this book are simple and direct. Two stand out above all:

There Are Stages on Our Journey

Caregivers report common milestones in the caregiving experience. These are the "seasons" in our caring for someone with AIDS. We've called them stages.

Knowing in advance what events and feelings commonly occur in the stages of the caregiving experience can help us in several ways. First, like any map of unfamiliar territory, the element of surprise is lessened. What's more, knowing about stages underscores another fact: We are not alone. Other people have traveled the caregiving path. We can learn from and share in their experience.

We Can Accept Our Life and the People We Care For

There are really no victims. As caregivers, our serenity need not depend on the external circumstances of our life: job, friendship, salary, possessions. Nor does our serenity need to be at the mercy of our loved one's health or illness. Instead, serenity comes not from trying to control events in the outside world but from choosing our reactions to those events. Toward this end, we can learn, work with our feelings, and take appropriate action. And as we do, we will accept ourselves and our loved ones with AIDS.

Someone we love has AIDS. This fact has changed our life forever. However, it does not dictate *how* our life will change. No event need dictate our responses. Someone we love has AIDS—now, how will we live? Rather than merely suffer life from this point on, we can create it. As caregivers, we can truly choose our next stage.

Moreover, we can remind ourselves that the person we care for is more than a condition, more than a diagnosis. The person with AIDS is a person first—not a problem to solve, not a predicament to fix. Perhaps, in the end, caregiving means only being present, listening, giving attention, loving, and remaining open. And in that state of mind, the answers will come to us in each moment, as we need them.

Endnotes

CHAPTER ONE: AIDS:
WHAT ABOUT THE CAREGIVERS?

1. *Holy Bible,* RSV (Philadelphia: Board of Publication of the Lutheran Church in America, 1952), Ruth 1:16–18.
2. *Twelve Steps and Twelve Traditions* (New York: Alcoholics Anonymous World Services, Inc., 1952), 99.
3. *Alcoholics Anonymous,* 3rd ed. (New York: Alcoholics Anonymous World Services, Inc., 1976), 60.
4. Melody Beattie, *Codependent No More* (Center City, Minn.: Hazelden Educational Materials, 1987), 31.
5. Melody Beattie, *Beyond Codependency: And Getting Better All the Time* (Center City, Minn.: Hazelden Educational Materials, 1989), 6.
6. Robert Subby and John Friel, "Codependency – A Paradoxical Dependency," in *Co-Dependency, An Emerging Issue* (Pompano Beach, Fla.: Health Communications, Inc., 1984), pp. 34–44.
7. Timmen Cermak, *Diagnosing and Treating Co-Dependence* (Minneapolis: Johnson Institute, 1986), 55–56.
8. Kahlil Gibran, *The Prophet* (New York: Alfred A. Knopf, 1989), 16.

CHAPTER THREE: STAGE ONE: DISCOVERING –
LEARNING THE PAINFUL TRUTH

1. Bill, "This Matter of Fear," *The Grapevine,* 18:8 (January 1962): 6.
2. Mic Hunter, *The Twelve Steps and Shame* (Center City, Minn.: Hazelden Educational Materials, 1988), 1.
3. Melody Beattie, *Beyond Codependency: And Getting Better All the Time* (Center City, Minn.: Hazelden Educational Materials, 1989), 107–108.

4. From a lecture by Claudia Black.
5. *Webster's Ninth New Collegiate Dictionary* (Springfield, Mass.: Merriam-Webster, 1983).

CHAPTER SEVEN: PHASE A—LEARNING

1. Sasha Alyson, ed., *You Can Do Something About AIDS* (Boston: The Stop AIDS Project, Inc., 1988), 34.
2. Ibid., 34–35.

CHAPTER EIGHT: PHASE B— WORKING WITH FEELINGS

1. Thomas Harris, M.D., *I'm OK—You're OK: A Practical Guide to Transactional Analysis* (New York: Harper & Row, 1969), 25.
2. Perry Tilleraas, *The Color of Light: Daily Meditations for All of Us Living with AIDS* (Center City, Minn.: Hazelden Educational Materials, 1988), January 16 meditation.
3. Ram Dass and Paul Gorman, *How Can I Help? Stories and Reflections on Service* (New York: Alfred A. Knopf, 1985), 68.

CHAPTER NINE: PHASE C—TAKING ACTION

1. *Alcoholics Anonymous*, 3rd ed. (New York: Alcoholics Anonymous World Services, Inc., 1976), 449.
2. Eccl. 3:1–5.
3. *Alcoholics Anonymous*, 60.
4. Adapted from Step Twelve of *Alcoholics Anonymous*, in *How It Works*, the HIVIES Manual (Glenview, Ill.: HIVIES, 1989), 13–16.
5. Ram Dass and Paul Gorman, *How Can I Help? Stories*

and Reflections on Service (New York: Alfred A. Knopf, 1985), 68.

6. George R. Melton with Wil Garcia, *Beyond AIDS: A Journey Into Healing* (Beverly Hills, Calif.: Brotherhood Press, 1988), 71.

7. Dass and Gorman, *How Can I Help?*, 88.

CHAPTER TEN: PHASE D—ACCEPTANCE

1. Ram Dass and Paul Gorman, *How Can I Help? Stories and Reflections on Service* (New York: Alfred A. Knopf, 1985), 59.

2. Dass and Gorman, *How Can I Help?*, 63.

3. Perry Tilleraas, *The Color of Light: Daily Meditations for All of Us Living with AIDS* (Center City, Minn.: Hazelden Educational Materials, 1988), June 27 meditation.

4. *Alcoholics Anonymous*, 3rd ed. (New York: Alcoholics Anonymous World Services, Inc., 1976), 12.

5. *Alcoholics Anonymous*, 59–60.

6. 1 Cor. 13:4–8.

7. Viktor Frankl, *Man's Search for Meaning: An Introduction to Logotherapy* (New York: Washington Square Press, 1963), 14.

8. George R. Melton with Wil Garcia, *Beyond AIDS: A Journey Into Healing* (Beverly Hills, Calif.: Brotherhood Press, 1988), 103.

Appendices

The Twelve Steps of Alcoholics Anonymous*

1. We admitted we were powerless over alcohol—that our lives had become unmanageable.
2. Came to believe that a Power greater than ourselves could restore us to sanity.
3. Made a decision to turn our will and our lives over to the care of God *as we understood Him.*
4. Made a searching and fearless moral inventory of ourselves.
5. Admitted to God, to ourselves, and to another human being the exact nature of our wrongs.
6. Were entirely ready to have God remove all these defects of character.
7. Humbly asked Him to remove our shortcomings.
8. Made a list of all persons we had harmed, and became willing to make amends to them all.
9. Made direct amends to such people wherever possible, except when to do so would injure them or others.
10. Continued to take personal inventory and when we were wrong promptly admitted it.
11. Sought through prayer and meditation to improve our conscious contact with God *as we understood Him,* praying only for knowledge of His will for us and the power to carry that out.
12. Having had a spiritual awakening as the result of these steps, we tried to carry this message to alcoholics, and to practice these principles in all our affairs.

---

*The Twelve Steps of A.A. are taken from *Alcoholics Anonymous,* 3rd. ed., published by A.A. World Services, Inc., New York, N.Y., 59–60. Reprinted with permission. Alcoholics Anonymous is for recovery from alcoholism, and Twelve Step programs patterned after A.A. address other problems.

213

APPENDIX TWO

The Twelve Steps for People with HIV Illness*

Rarely have we seen a person lose hope who has thoroughly followed our path. Due to the seriousness of our virus, our primary purpose must be to band together with a great desire to live. United together because of this virus, we develop a strong bond with each other and make a decision to become as healthy as humanly possible in mind, body, and spirit. Those who are not willing to try this program are usually men and women who have made a decision to surrender to the despair and hopelessness of our infection. There are such unfortunates. They have succumbed to the hysteria and misinformation surrounding HIV. At this point, there is no cure. We need help in learning how to avoid or minimize high-risk behavior as well as maintain a positive attitude. For some of us, this change is very difficult.

Our stories disclose, in a general way, what our behaviors used to be like, and how we became aware of our infections, and what we are doing to change our high-risk behaviors.

If you have made a decision to live with hope rather than succumb to the despair and are willing to go to any length to get it, then you are ready to take certain steps.

At some of these we balked. We thought we could continue our old behavior patterns, but we cannot. With all the earnestness at our command, we beg of you to be fearless and thorough from the very start. Some of us have tried to hold onto our old ideas and behaviors, and the result was nil until we let go absolutely.

Remember that we deal with HIV infection—hopeless,

---

*Adapted from Chapter Five of *Alcoholic Anonymous*, taken from *How it Works*, the HIVIES Manual. Reprinted with permission. For more information, write to HIVIES, 610 Greenwood, Glenview, Illinois 60025.

frightening, powerful. Without help, it is too much for us, but there is one who has all power. That one is God. May you find God now.

Half measures availed us nothing. We stood at the turning point. We asked God's protection with complete abandon.

Here are the Steps we took which are suggested as a program of recovery:*

1. We admitted we are infected with HIV and our lives have become unmanageable.
2. Came to believe that a Power greater than ourselves can guide us to healthy behavior.
3. Made a decision to turn our wills and lives over to the care of God, as we understood God.
4. Made a searching and fearless moral inventory of ourselves, to identify high-risk behaviors we may be practicing.
5. Admitted to God, to ourselves, and to another human being the exact nature of our unhealthy behavior patterns we need to change.
6. Were entirely ready to have God remove our unhealthy behaviors.
7. Humbly asked God to remove our unhealthy behaviors.
8. Made a list of all persons we had harmed and became willing to make amends to them all, thereby minimizing stress and discomfort in our lives.
9. Made direct amends to such people wherever possible except when to do so would injure them or others.
10. Continued to take personal inventory and when we did choose to use high-risk behaviors, promptly admitted it and sought to change our patterns.
11. Sought through prayer, meditation, nutrition, and exercise to improve our conscious contact with God as

---

*Adapted from the Twelve Steps of Alcoholics Anonymous.

we understood God, praying only for knowledge of God's will for us and the power to carry that out.

12. Having had a spiritual awakening as the result of these steps, we tried to carry this message to other HIV infected people, and to practice these principles in all our affairs.

APPENDIX THREE

Basic Information on AIDS

Caitlin Ryan, M.S.W., and Melvin Pohl, M.D.

An excerpt from Protocol for AIDS Education and Risk Reduction Counseling in Chemical Dependency Treatment Settings, *copyright 1989 by ARC Research Foundation, 12300 Twinbrook Parkway, Suite 150, Rockville, MD 20852, (301) 816–9700. Used here with permission.*

Every minute, somewhere in the world, another person is diagnosed with a deadly, incurable illness: acquired immunodeficiency syndrome (AIDS). In the United States, some two million other persons are infected with and capable of transmitting AIDS through intimate sexual contact and needle-sharing behaviors. Still others suffer from AIDS-related conditions or fear and anxiety associated with possible exposure to AIDS.

AIDS is an epidemic. It has the potential to affect all aspects of our daily lives. By 1991, approximately 270,000 Americans will have been diagnosed with AIDS, and 1.1 million will be diagnosed worldwide. Within the next ten years, 1 million cases of AIDS are projected in the U.S. alone, with several million more expected throughout the world.

AIDS has been reported in 152 countries. Today in some central African countries, 25 percent of the adult population is already infected; another 25 percent of the diagnosed cases of AIDS are among children. In the United States, human immunodeficiency virus (HIV) infection has and will continue to increase among heterosexuals who use IV drugs, their sexual partners, and their children. AIDS is currently one of the five leading causes of death among children ages one through five. More than 70 percent of their parents either use IV drugs or were a sexual partner of an IV-drug user. In New York City, AIDS is the leading cause of death among women ages twenty-five through twenty-nine years old—more than half of whom are IV-drug users—and 53 percent of cases in New York City have occurred in IV-drug users. In San Francisco, the rate of HIV infection among IV-drug users increased by 50 percent in one year. In New Jersey, one out of every seventy-five residents is infected with HIV and in some high-incidence cities, this rate increases to one in four.

AIDS does not discriminate on the basis of sex, age, race, ethnic origin, sexual orientation, geographic location, income, or level of education. AIDS is not transmitted by casual contact. Most important, AIDS is preventable: education and information are our best defense against AIDS.

* * * * *

AIDS (Acquired Immunodeficiency Syndrome) is the most serious epidemic facing our society today. Although scattered cases occurred prior to this time, AIDS was first recognized in a group of gay men in 1981, and since that time, over 100,000 cases have been reported nationwide, including more than 58,000 deaths. There are an estimated 700,000 cases worldwide. By the end of this century, it is estimated that more than 1 million people will have died from AIDS, with 5–10 million people having been infected worldwide in the 1980s alone. Three times that number will become infected before the end of the century, and at least one third of those infections are preventable.

AIDS is an underlying disorder of the immune system caused by the human immunodeficiency virus (HIV); the virus used to be identified as HTLV-III. In individuals who become infected, HIV acts as a slow, silent virus. Once infected with this virus, the body's ability to fight off infection may become drastically impaired. As a result, infected individuals whose immune systems become sufficiently damaged eventually develop infections caused by germs and bacteria that do not affect people with normally functioning immune systems. Individuals with AIDS tend to develop unusual types of pneumonias or other protozoal, viral, fungal, or bacterial opportunistic infections, as well as unusual and rare forms of cancers. They also develop unusual skin infections, brain infections, and other malignancies.

To date, there may be as many as 500,000 individuals who have developed what is sometimes referred to as HIV-spectrum disease or AIDS-related complex (ARC), although there are no reliable figures for this diagnostic category. ARC is a less severe disorder caused by infection with HIV and characterized by some AIDS-related symptoms that may appear in mild, moderate, or severe forms. According to our current knowledge, perhaps 30 percent of individuals with ARC will go on to develop AIDS over the course of seven years.

To receive a diagnosis of AIDS, the patient, in addition to being infected with HIV, must have one of the following: (1) presumptive or proven opportunistic infection, (2) one of several forms of cancer, (3) HIV encephalopathy (problems with thinking, judgment, memory, mood, and other brain functions) with resulting cognitive dysfunction, or (4) wasting syndrome with weight loss, fever, and diarrhea.

The clinical course of HIV-spectrum disease varies for people who are infected with HIV. Initially, infection appears typically like a viral illness with fever, swollen glands, and body aches. After the initial infection, the virus will commonly enter special cells of the body's immune system (T-4 lymphocytes) and become dormant, often for a period of time (ten years or more in some people). This period of dormancy is referred to as the "incubation period."

In some people, HIV continues to reproduce within T-cells and other immune cells until the virus eventually damages the person's ability to fight off infections or cancer. For some who are infected, general signs of damage to the immune system may appear, including fevers, night sweats, diarrhea, or mild infections such as thrush. ARC develops in others, and includes some of the signs already mentioned as well as fatigue, swollen glands, weight loss, and blood abnormalities. Still others become ill from infections or cancers that are progressive, serious, and debilitating. In the worst of cases they may be fatal.

HIV is spread between humans through intimate sexual contact (by the entry of semen or vaginal fluid into the blood stream) or by the exchange of blood. It is unlikely that enough virus is present in tears, saliva, or sweat to permit transmission of this virus between two people through these "body fluids," and even if enough virus were present, direct access to the blood stream is required before infection with HIV can occur. To date, no cases have been reported of infection with HIV through casual contact, even in studies of family members who have shared eating utensils, bathrooms, and common household areas, and who have had recurrent, nonsexual contact with body fluids of people with HIV infection.

In the U.S., the most recent CDC [Centers for Disease Control] HIV surveillance data indicate that 61 percent of the cases of AIDS are in gay or bisexual men. Twenty-eight percent of cases have occurred in IV-drug users (7 percent of cases are in gay, male IV-drug users). Approximately 5 percent of the cases of AIDS are reported to be caused by heterosexual contact, and it is anticipated that this figure will increase by 9 percent within the next five years.

TREATMENT

To date, there is no effective cure for AIDS and no vaccine to prevent infection with HIV. Though researchers are actively pursuing a variety of strategies at present, medical science is limited in its treatment options.

Zidovudine (Retrovir)®, known as AZT, is the first federally approved drug that prolongs the lives of people with AIDS and ARC. AZT prevents HIV from reproducing in human cells, but it does not directly kill HIV. Many other drug therapies are being investigated, including those that decrease the activity of the virus (antivirals) and those that stimulate the immune system to fight infection (immune enhancers). There are also ongoing investigations into the effects of AZT on HIV-infected people who have normal or low-normal T-cell counts and no symptoms of illness. Results of these investigations have suggested that early treatment with AZT can prevent further breakdown of the immune system and prevent progression of HIV infection to AIDS in people with fewer than 500 T-4 cells. For this and other related reasons, the CDC has recommended HIV testing and regular T-cell testing for all who suspect they are at high risk for HIV infection.

In the last several years, improved diagnostic and therapeutic techniques for treating opportunistic infections have prolonged the survival of many people with AIDS. Among the techniques are effective drug protocols to treat *Pneumocystis carinii* pneumonia, the most common of the potentially fatal HIV-related infections. Several experimental protocols are available to prevent infection in people with depressed immunity. These include treatment with prophylactic Bactrim® (Trimethoprim-Sulfamethoxazole®) and inhaled Pentamadine (Lyphomed®) which should be made available to all patients with AIDS and evidence of immune dysfunction (fewer than 200 T-4 cells).

Worldwide, it is estimated that several million people are

already infected with HIV, and a high proportion of these people possess antibodies to HIV. The presence of antibodies in the blood indicates that the immune system has met the virus and has attempted to fight it. At the current time, it is possible to test routinely only for antibodies to HIV. The issues related to testing will be discussed more thoroughly in a later section.

Symptoms of AIDS include evidence of viral infection such as weight loss, fatigue, night sweats, fever, lymph-node swelling, diarrhea; evidence of cognitive dysfunction (difficulty in thinking); symptoms of opportunistic infection (shortness of breath, skin rashes, mouth infections, changes in blood count) and symptoms of cancer (purplish spots on the skin, unusual lumps or bumps, or bleeding from internal lesions). If any of these symptoms develop and persist, the patient must consult a knowledgeable physician immediately for an evaluation. Symptoms of cognitive dysfunction may also be present in people with chronic drug dependency or alcoholism as a result of chemical usage. Therefore, both HIV and chemical dependency should be considered as possible causes of cognitive dysfunction.

SAFER-SEX GUIDELINES

Since HIV is transmitted sexually as well as through the exchange of blood, it is extremely important to know the recommended guidelines for safer sex in order to reduce the risk of passing infection, becoming infected, or being re-infected. Sexually active gay or bisexual men, gay and heterosexual intravenous drug users who have shared needles, and their sexual partners have a high probability of already having been exposed to HIV. Those involved in AIDS education efforts are now identifying higher-risk behaviors instead of high-risk groups. It is these behaviors that place individuals at risk for infection with HIV. Thus, any sexually active individual with a number of sexual partners must be informed of AIDS transmission and risk-reduction behaviors.

Merely presenting information is not enough to bring about behavioral change. In order to change behavior, people need to: (1) identify the risk as real and personalize it, (2) implement the following guidelines, and (3) receive support for behavior change, preferably in ongoing support groups.

The following sexual behaviors have been classified according to their level of risk by the Bay Area Physicians for Human Rights.

SAFER: mutual masturbation, dry kissing, body massage and rubbing, using one's own sex toys.

POSSIBLY SAFER: insertive anal intercourse with a condom, fellatio (sucking) before climax, wet kissing, vaginal intercourse with a condom, oral-vaginal contact, having body contact with urine or feces, receptive anal intercourse with a condom (using spermicidal gel with Nonoxynol 9).

UNSAFE: receptive anal intercourse without a condom, insertive anal intercourse without a condom, fisting (inserting hand into anus or vagina), fellatio (sucking), oral-anal contact (rimming), vaginal intercourse without a condom, swallowing urine or feces.

These guidelines reflect our current knowledge as to which sexual behaviors may be safer than others. However, the correct term for such practices is *safer* rather than *safe*, since one can never be certain of the long-term effects of any behavior, nor of other important factors that affect transmission, such as frequency of contact, dose of the virus, other infections, and susceptibility of the individual.

AIDS AND CHEMICAL DEPENDENCY

It is absolutely critical for individuals with the diseases of chemical dependency and alcoholism to be well informed about AIDS. It is particularly important for gay men to realize that a gay male drug user, especially if he has used intravenous drugs, is at highest risk for having been exposed to HIV.

In addition, there are some theories which suggest that infection with HIV alone is not sufficient to cause an individual to develop AIDS. There may be certain "cofactors" that combine to cause damage to the immune system along with HIV. Perhaps the most commonly suspected cofactors that can damage the immune system are alcohol and drugs. Alcohol, marijuana, amyl and butyl nitrite (poppers), and perhaps opiates and PCP may damage the body's immune system. It is hypothesized that substance use and exposure to HIV may combine to cause AIDS to develop in infected individuals. Furthermore, research has shown that HIV may be more likely to infect the T-cells of people who use drugs like alcohol and cocaine. Stahl, et al., found that people, when using alcohol, marijuana, and other depressant drugs, have been shown to practice unsafe and risky behaviors despite knowledge of the dangers of these behaviors. This can be particularly true if, under the influence of depressant drugs, blackouts occur, since at these times people can neither remember nor account for their behavior. Obviously, if both exposure to the virus and drug or alcohol dependency are risk factors, these behaviors must be thoroughly reviewed with all patients regardless of their sexual orientation. Furthermore, it is speculated that repeated exposure to drugs, alcohol, and HIV may increase the possibility of developing AIDS, suggesting that changing behaviors can reduce risk.

The demographic profile of people with AIDS is now changing. Gay and bisexual men and IV-drug users and their partners have been at highest risk for infection with HIV because the virus has been transmitted largely within these groups since 1977. Because gay men have been particularly affected, many experts have suggested that gay men should consider themselves as already being infected with the virus. Since they are assumed to have already been infected, it is recommended that gay and bisexual men and others who have engaged in risky behaviors refrain from donating blood, sperm, and organs, always practice safer sex, and boost their health and nutritional status through proper exercise and diet. With the availability of more effective treatment to prevent the development of infections and future deterioration of their immune systems, many providers and community AIDS workers are recognizing that gay men and IV-drug users take an HIV-antibody test, and if positive, have their T-cells checked regularly.

HIV-ANTIBODY TEST

The HIV test most commonly used is the ELISA test, developed to test for the presence of antibodies to HIV. This test uses a color-sensitive chemical that changes color to a greater or lesser degree when antibodies present in a patient's blood sample come into contact with a preparation containing HIV. In general, the test is given a second time for each blood sample that reacts during the first round of testing. Samples that react twice to the ELISA test are then tested with a more sophisticated follow-up blood test called the Western Blot test. If the Western Blot test is positive, there is little doubt that the person has antibodies to HIV.

It is not uncommon to have a positive ELISA test result in persons who do not have antibodies to HIV in their blood. These are called "false positive" tests. The accuracy of screening blood for the presence of antibodies is high if both tests are used. However, false positive results do happen. The full meaning of a positive finding is a critical issue in counseling individuals who take the test. It is essential to confirm a positive ELISA test with a follow-up Western Blot test before assuming a person is truly positive.

Since the test only identifies antibodies to HIV, the clinician can neither tell which individuals are actually carrying the virus, nor identify those who are capable of infecting others and those who are not. Anyone who tests positive must be presumed capable of transmitting the virus.

Once an individual has been infected with HIV (some individuals have tested positive after only one contact), antibodies will begin to develop. It is estimated that antibodies will develop in most people during a time period that extends from three weeks to six months following infection. In a small number of individuals, it has taken as long as twelve to eighteen months for antibodies to develop. The incidence of false negative tests is rare, but, in some circumstances, a person may be infected with HIV, not have antibodies, and have a negative test.

Several cases of transfusion-associated HIV infection have been reported that involve individuals who tested negative for antibodies at the time they donated blood. Because antibodies did not develop until after donated blood was transfused, some individuals became infected from the transfusion. Today, the chances of becoming infected through a blood transfusion are estimated 1 in 50,000.

There are several newer methods to test for evidence of infection with HIV that measure the presence of the virus itself or antigen rather than antibodies. Antigen usually appears early after infection and disappears within a few months. Later, if the virus is activated, the dormancy ends, and antigen levels rise. A rising antigen level is typically associated with deterioration of a person's physical condition and may indicate the development of AIDS in a person who previously had no symptoms. Antigen tests are still relatively experimental and expensive. A newer test called the PCR (Polymerase Chain Reaction) has been developed to detect HIV antigen. Not yet routinely available, it is still being standardized for interpretation in general use. When available commercially, this test will be able to confirm antibody tests and assist physicians in making diagnostic and treatment decisions.

* * * * *

From a strictly infectious disease standpoint, abstaining from sexual contact during the current health crisis is the safest strategy. Since sexual abstinence is uncommon for most individuals, it is important to underscore the risks of certain sexual behaviors and to provide alternatives that reduce risk. Giving no alternatives may increase the individual's frustration and tendency to act out sexually, with drugs, or both.

APPENDIX FOUR

Recommended Materials on AIDS and Caregiving

Adair, Margo, and Lynn Johnson. *Visualization and AIDS*. San Francisco: Tool for Change, 1985.

Eidson, Ted, ed. *The AIDS Caregiver's Handbook*. New York: St. Martin's Press, 1988.

Gawain, Shakti. *Living in the Light*. San Rafael, Calif.: Whatever Publications, 1986.

Hay, Louise L. *You Can Heal Your Life*. Santa Monica, Calif.: Hay House, 1984.

Kushner, Harold S. *When Bad Things Happen to Good People*. New York: Shocken Books, 1981.

Martelli, Leonard, with Fran Peltz and William Messina. *When Someone You Know Has AIDS: A Practical Guide*. New York: Crown, 1987.

Melton, George R., with Wil Garcia. *Beyond AIDS: A Journey Into Healing*. Beverly Hills, Calif.: Brotherhood Press, 1988.

Moffat, Betty Clare. *When Someone You Love Has AIDS: A Book of Hope for Family and Friends*. New York: NAL Penguin, 1986.

Ram Dass, and Paul Gorman. *How Can I Help?* New York: Alfred A Knopf, 1985.

Siegel, Bernie S., M.D. *Love, Medicine, & Miracles*. San Francisco: Harper and Row, 1987.

Siegel, Larry, M.D., and Milan Korcok. *AIDS: The Drug and Alcohol Connection.* Center City, Minn.: Hazelden Educational Materials, 1989.

Simonton, Carl O., et al. *Getting Well Again.* New York: Bantam Books, 1984.

Tilleraas, Perry. *The Color of Light: Daily Meditations for All of Us Living with AIDS.* Center City, Minn.: Hazelden Educational Materials, 1988.

Index

A

Acceptance. *See* Phase D: Acceptance
Adapting. *See* Stage Two: Adapting
Adult children of alcoholics, 8
Affirmations, 179–181
AIDS. *See also* Phase A: Learning
  basic information on, 216–226
  caregiver and, 7–8
  chemical dependency and, 7, 10–11
  prevalence of, 7
  telling others about, 68–69
  unique aspects for caregivers, 9
AL 721, 86
Al-Anon, 8
Alateen, 8
Alcoholics Anonymous, 8, 10, 53, 169, 174, 190
Anger, 56–59
Anxiety, 64–65
AZT, 85

B

Beyond AIDS: A Journey Into Healing, 181
Beyond Codependency: And Getting Better All the Time, 62
Bible, 8–9, 161, 172, 200
Black, Claudia, 62
Blame, 67–68
Book of Ecclesiastes, 172
Burnout, 182–184
But for the grace of God, go I, 149–50

E

Easy does it, 149
Expectations vs. expectancies, 147–148

F

False guilt, 62, 64
Fear, 53–56
Feelings. *See also* Phase B: Working with Feelings
  alleviating negative feelings, 21
  in Stage One, 51–53
Forgiveness, 195
Frankl, Viktor, 200–201

G

Garcia, Wil, 181
Get a sponsor, 150
Gibran, Kahlil, 17–18
God, 150–151, 191–192, 196–197
Gorman, Paul, 160–161, 175, 184, 188
Gratitude, 194–195
Guilt, 62–63

H

Harris, Thomas, 139
Hay, Louise, 181
Higher Power, 150–151, 191–192, 196–199
How Can I Help? 175, 184, 188
Hypervigilance, 14–15

I

"I" messages, 163–164

P

T

238